PEARL HARBOR

From Fishponds to Warships

PEARL HARBOR

A COMPLETE ILLUSTRATED HISTORY

By Allan Seiden

Mutual Publishing

Softcover: ISBN 1-56647-505-8
Hardcover: ISBN 1-56647-511-2

Library of Congress Catalog Card
Number: 2001089905

First Printing, May 2001
1 2 3 4 5 6 7 8 9

Mutual Publishing
1215 Center Street, Suite 210
Honolulu, Hawaii 96816
Telephone (808) 732-1709
Fax (808) 734-4094
e-mail: mutual@lava.net
www.mutualpublishing.com

Printed in Korea

DEDICATION

Dedicated to all those who have fallen in defense of our freedoms. First, to the 2,500 people who lost their lives at Pearl Harbor on December 7, 1941. Second, to the generation of which they were a part, for its willingness to sacrifice for the common good and to fight all the necessary battles. Men like my father, for whom this book is personally dedicated. Special thanks go to my publisher, Bennett Hymer for his love of books and the look of the past. To Jane Hopkins for focused oversight and Sistenda Yim for providing the lovely design of the pages that follow. To Judi Bowman, curator at the U.S. Army Museum of Hawai'i, for her many invaluable leads. To DeSoto Brown, archivist at the Bishop Museum, for his professional help on several levels. To Tom Shaw, Executive Director of the *Arizona* Memorial Museum Association for his generous sharing of Tom Freeman's exciting Pearl Harbor art; Daniel Martinez, USS *Arizona* Memorial Historian, for his suggestions and facilitation; and to Stan Melman, USS *Arizona* Memorial Photo Archivist, whose kind help made my work easier. Lastly, my appreciation to Bianka Fietz and Veronica Carmona for their motivating interest and kind support.

Allan Seiden
Honolulu, March, 2001

TABLE OF CONTENTS

INTRODUCTION

There are places and events of such singular significance that they are part of both personal history and national identity. Pearl Harbor is such a place.

Indelible memories link Americans to Pearl Harbor. It is a place of pilgrimage not only for the generation that fought in World War II, but also for their descendants, in some families into the fourth post-war generation. Pearl Harbor has also become a place of pilgrimage for people of countries drawn into the maelstrom of war, including hundreds of thousands of Japanese.

Pearl Harbor is now a healing place, a place of *mana,* as the Hawaiians call spiritual power. A visit creates a lingering silence, a meditative evaluation of war and idealism, loss and rebirth, faith and the sacrifice life sometimes demands. In this it offers a universal message that truly honors all those lost that day.

A visit starts at the USS *Arizona* Memorial Visitor Center. Operated by the National Park Service, it provides an excellent orientation, via museum displays and film that are both first rate.

Granted to the U.S. in negotiations with the Hawaiian government related to the import of Hawaiian sugar in 1888, Pearl Harbor grew in importance over the years, making a quantum leap when the U.S. headquartered its Pacific Fleet here in 1940. By 1941, Hawai`i was on a war footing, although few anticipated the timing or impact of events that would make December 7, 1941 a date remembered by people around the world.

So profound was the outcome of the attack on Pearl Harbor that it remains Hawai'i's premier visitor attraction. Each year nearly 1.6-million people make their way to the USS *Arizona* Memorial Visitor Center. It is not only Americans who come to pay homage, but also Japanese for whom this place has an equally compelling message. As it was a date burned into the national consciousness of the United States, so too was it a milestone for Japan—for the war that ensued from this precipitous attack would ultimately result in a defeat so complete as to strip Japan of much of its past.

It was Japan's attack on Pearl Harbor that made this isolated port on O'ahu's southern coast a familiar name. Newspapers around the world carried the news of the attack, with maps and pictures that vividly and tragically introduced Pearl Harbor to the outside world.

Yet today Pearl Harbor is a symbol of perseverance and courage. It is the story of a generation that sacrificed for the common good and bravely brought victory from disaster. But first, let's pull back the curtain on an earlier time. A time before the first human eyes had yet to see Hawai`i. It is here that the story begins.

Morning light over Pearl Harbor and the Wai'anae Mountains in a painting by Joseph Strong done in 1889 when it was still a primeval wetland.

CHAPTER ONE
·
A TROPICAL LAGOON

Cocoanut Lagoon,
Hawaii.

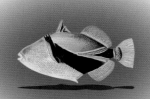

A TROPICAL LAGOON

Situated on the south-central O'ahu coast, further from the mountains than anyplace on the island, there was a great lagoon. It was a landmark presence, with two large bays that were a haven for many species of birds, fish, and other creatures that had made their way here over the eons, adapting to its wetland environment and flourishing.

To the Hawaiians it was known as Pu'uloa, but by the mid-19th century it would come to be called Pearl Harbor.

A broad expanse of more than 20 square miles, Pu'uloa's waters were fed by rains that fell over the Ko'olau and Wai'anae ranges, as well as by tidal surges that entered the lagoon through a passage that led to the open sea.

Although mountains rose in the distance, the sky was the dominant

Meandering streams and grassy wetlands made Pearl Harbor a congenial home to many species of birds, including native plovers and stilts.

reality, hanging over the flat wetlands in sun-charged blues. Well in the lee of O'ahu's mountains, little rain fell over Pearl Harbor, the clouds drained of moisture long before they drifted this far from O'ahu's inland summits.

If rainfall alone were the determining factor, this rich wetland might be deemed a desert. On the contrary, it was richly alive, a place where nature's abundance would provide sustenance to the Native Hawaiians.

Few trees grew in the water-saturated soil, much of it brackish. Pu'uloa was defined by grasses, sedge, mangrove, and dense thickets of marsh. This was a borderland, a place where sea and land lived in intricate balance.

These coastal lands were mostly made of limestone, evidence of

The *'alae ke'oke'o* and the *pennula euadata* were at home in the wetlands. Some birds nested and lived here, while others used it as a source of food.

countless years when a higher sea inundated much of today's coastal lowlands. Coral flourished in the warm, shallow waters. In the passing of uncounted millennia, limestone, created by soft-bodied corals as a home, capped the lava rock that originally formed Oʻahu.

As the sea retreated, perhaps as recently as 10,000 years ago, Puʻuloa took the clover-like shape that the world would one day come to recognize as Pearl Harbor.

The waters of this expansive lagoon were divided into three bays created by two irregular peninsula's projecting into the water from the northern flatlands. The three bays, later to be called lochs, were linked to the sea by a single narrow channel. The waters within the lagoon ranged from muddy shallows to 40-foot depths.

There were also a number of islands within the lagoon. Some were merely sandy spits inundated at high tide. Others were permanent, providing a haven for nesting birds.

Fresh water continuously trickled in from the mountains, often surfacing in bubbling springs. The

From the foothills of the Waiʻanae Mountains, the wetlands of Pearl Harbor spread out in lush abundance.

lagoon's waters were also cleansed and replenished by the ebb and flow of tidal seas. The resulting mix of fresh water and sea water provided a congenial home to species at home in either element. That included the small oysters that made the pearls that would one day give this primeval wilderness a name. But first there would be a thousand-year span when Polynesians were a daily part of the life of this wetland landscape. ■

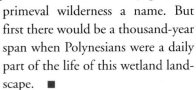

The Reverend William Ellis did this hand-colored engraving of Pearl Harbor and the 'Ewa plains in the 1820s.

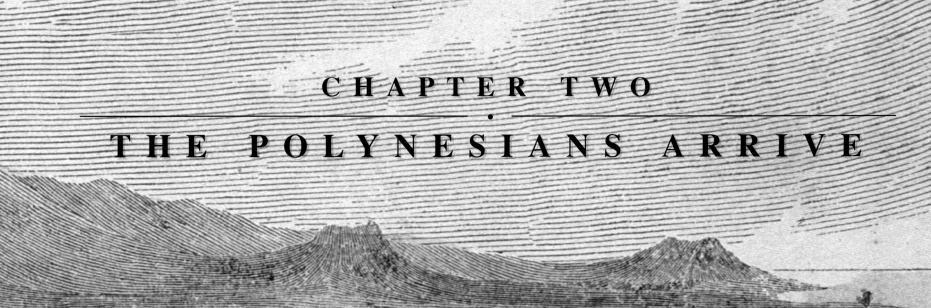

CHAPTER TWO
·
THE POLYNESIANS ARRIVE

Two *kanaka maoli*, Native Hawaiian men, harvesting Pearl's wetland sedge for use in thatching roofs of traditional Hawaiian *hale*, circa 1895.

THE POLYNESIANS ARRIVE

From the open sea, Pearl Harbor's broad lochs would have remained hidden from view. Only a shallow channel, less than a mile wide, hinted of the sheltered waters that lay beyond. Reading the clouds and their reflection on the sea, scrutinizing the coastal landscape, noting the species of birds and sea life, the Hawaiians would have quickly drawn the conclusion that this was a place that invited further scrutiny.

Heading toward shore, they first reached a reef-shallowed passage that revealed this newly discovered world as a place of abundance. For outrigger paddlers used to the churning waters of the open sea, a paddle in Pu'uloa provided a peaceful idyll, although its waters could get choppy when the wind came up.

It remains uncertain just when the period of settlement began, or the path of colonization that followed. Perhaps Pu'uloa was quick to attract the attention of these Polynesian settlers. Perhaps it was not until some time had passed that they became aware of the rich bounty it offered.

Sheltered from the open sea, this great lagoon provided a home to a variety of fish, including both freshwater and saltwater species. There were many other forms of sea life, plus wild duck and other tempting bird species to supplement the diet. The tall sedge and grasses were valued in roofing homes and in weaving.

Voyaging canoes, like the one pictured by artist Herb Kāne, brought the first Polynesians to Hawai'i's shores. The outrigger canoe, or *wa'a*, provided both transportation and a means of fishing the reef and open ocean. (Below and above)

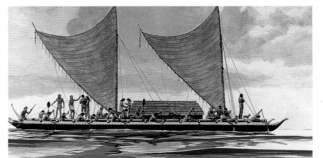

The Hawaiians knew of the tiny pearls grown by oysters abundant in Pu'uloa's calm, nutrient-rich waters. Small and irregular in shape and color, these pearls were not highly valued by the Hawaiians, who found other resources far more worthy of their attention. As with Diamond Head, where British soldiers thought the glint of calcite crystals to be that of diamonds, outsiders would see Pu'uloa's pearls as its most valuable asset. By the mid-19th century, the name Pearl Harbor had widely replaced Pu'uloa.

Although rich with potential, the wetland environment was not conducive to settlement. Most who came to Pu'uloa lived elsewhere, most likely along the 'Ewa or Wai'anae coasts, or inland where taro was grown.

Numerous fishponds were built along Pu'uloa's meandering coastline. With sheltered waters, extensive shallows, and a steady supply of fresh water, Pu'uloa was designed for Hawaiian aquaculture. Here and there were simple *hale* (houses) for the guardians of the fishponds, who kept a daily vigil, not only maintaining the ponds, but also assuring no loss of fish to thieves or free-roaming pigs and dogs.

Few places in the Islands had a greater concentration of fishponds. Archeological surveys reveal no fewer than 27 ponds, most adjacent to the coast, called *loko kuapā,*

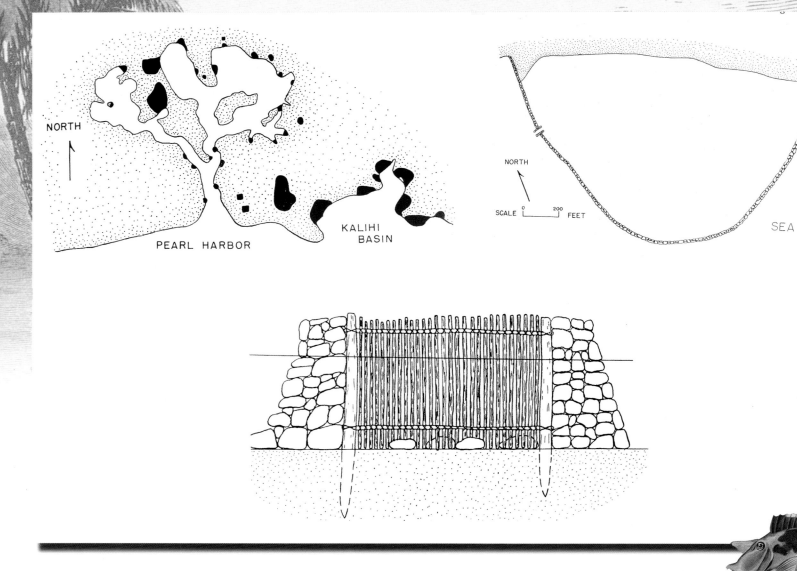

Pearl Harbor's extensive shallows, with their brackish waters, offered a setting conducive to Hawaiian aquaculture. *Pu'uloa,* as the Hawaiians called this great lagoon, had one of the largest concentrations of fishponds, or *loko i'a,* anywhere in Hawai'i. The *loko kuapā* (right), or walled fishpond, was one of several types found at *Pu'uloa.* The *makaha,* or gate, prevented larger fish from exiting the fishpond.

a few inland, called *loko 'umeiki*. There were fishponds of all sizes, some as smaller than an acre, some as large as 200 acres.

The *loko kuapā* were generally built by connecting two points of land with a rock wall from three to five feet tall and three to four feet wide. Built of coral rock or basalt or a combination of the two, the wall was broken by one or more gates, called *makaha,* actually the name of the wooden barricade that blocked the opening. Tidal waters flowed freely through the *makaha,* cleaning the pond at low tide and replenishing it as the high tide returned.

Naturally stocked by the open sea, the *loko i'a* were also filled with specially prized fish caught in the open ocean or on the reefs. With some species, fry were captured where streams met the ocean. The ponds, with their warm, shallow, brackish waters were rich with algae that quickly fattened the pond's *i'a,* as the Hawaiians called fish.

The *loko kuapā* were maintained and harvested for the benefit of the *ali'i,* the ruling chiefs. Communal effort over the span of a year went into the construction of many ponds. With walls as long as 5,000 feet, the fishponds were major construction projects requiring the concerted effort of whole communities. Only chiefly power could ensure their construction. The earliest surveyed pond dates back to the mid-1400s, although it is likely smaller ponds may well have been built earlier. Hundreds of *loko i'a* were built over the centuries that followed, a timeframe that matched the *ali'i* rise to power.

There were also smaller freshwater ponds just inland of the coast. Called *loko wai,* they were natural pools that were fed by the underground flow of water from the mountains. In some cases these natural ponds might be enlarged. Author Emma Beckley wrote of *loko wai* she saw in 1883:

Kala, Humuhumu and *Kupoupou* were amongst the numerous fish raised in royal fishponds. (opposite and below)

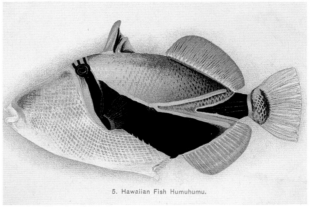

5. Hawaiian Fish Humuhumu.

"Fresh water ponds are very seldom over half an acre in extent and are for 'o'opu and 'opae preserves, and sometimes for awa, a kind of tropical salmon that breeds in brackish water and will live and grow fat in perfectly fresh water. The young fry of these fish, procured in shallow waters on the beach where a stream or spring or fresh water mingle with the sea, and are carried in gourds, more than a mile inland."

By 1850, with the Native Hawaiian population in decline, the era of fishponds was fast fading to memory. In time, most fell into disrepair, filling with silt, their rock walls slowly damaged.

Others outside the Islands, however, would eye Pearl Harbor's sheltered waters with a new use in mind. In an age in which navies helped make empires, Pearl Harbor would tempt those who calculated its value in military terms to an imperial age.

Claus Spreckels, a leading plantation owner and refiner, stated the obvious in describing Pearl Harbor's value. His 1880s evaluation was a prediction that would prove only partially accurate:

"The power which holds Pearl Harbor…will be mistress of the seas of the north Pacific. The possession of Pearl Harbor as a naval station has been guaranteed to the United States government by treaty for a number of years. Why not improve the harbor and make this condition of occupation perpetual by treaty conferring perpetual reciprocal advantages upon Hawai'i…This should not, and, indeed, need not involve any attack upon the independence of the Islands. No one could be more opposed to their annexation to the United States than I am." ■

KALĀKAUA, RECIPROCITY & PEARL HARBOR

The expansion of Europe's overseas empires, a process in motion since the late 15th century, would draw Hawai'i into the eco-political web of the world's leading powers by the early 19th century. Hawai'i's value lay in its location at the heart of the Pacific, in its sheltered harbors and anchorages, and in the provisions it could provide ships en route across the Pacific. By the 1840s, Great Britain, France, and the United States were already embroiled in disputes related to their actions toward the Kingdom of Hawai'i. For most of the 19th century a precarious balance prevailed, with Hawaiian independence in jeopardy on several occasions.

While Great Britain and France already had large, well-established overseas empires, the United States, itself a British colony until 1776, had spent its imperial energy in conquering the Indian tribes that blocked its transcontinental expansion. Now with that phase of nation-building accomplished, America began to look overseas.

Although it was the British who first reached the Hawaiian Islands with Captain James Cook's arrival in 1778, within 50 years American influence was predominant. Initially it was less a matter of political power than the on-site influence of whalers starting in 1819, the New England missionaries starting in the 1820s, and businessmen and traders who arrived in the 1840s and 50s. It was also Hawai'i's "proximity" to the United States, which created an economic link between the two that could not be matched by any of the European powers.

By the 1870s, plantation agriculture had emerged as the backbone of the Hawaiian economy. This gave the planters and their companies a powerful voice in formulating government policy. That led to a reciprocity treaty with the United States that would allow Hawaiian sugar and molasses to enter the U.S. duty-free.

At first the reciprocity treaty was fought for on its

Pearl Harbor remained a lovely wetland during the years of the Hawaiian monarchy, although by the late 19th century, most of its fishponds had been abandoned.

own merits, as an economic incentive that would benefit both Hawai'i and the United States. In time, as the royal government grew ever more dependent on plantation agriculture's revenues and America sought to expand its influence overseas, reciprocity would become linked to Pearl Harbor.

Sugar-cane fields bordered Pearl Harbor's northern and western shores by the 1870s. The free access of Hawaiian sugar to the U.S. linked Pearl Harbor's sheltered waters to reciprocity.

There were those, including King Kalākaua and his sister Lili'uokalani, who succeeded him on the throne in 1891, who thought that linking reciprocity to extraterritorial rights to Pearl Harbor set a dangerous precedent. Preserving Hawaiian independence had been a hard-fought battle since the 1840s. Ceding lands, sacred to Hawaiian tradition, was seen as paving the way for annexation.

Kalākaua had not been the first to fear that outcome. There had been opposition to reciprocity since it had first been broached in the 1850s, during the reign of Kamehameha IV. There was also resistance to reciprocity in the American Congress, where Louisiana sugar interests were particularly vocal in their opposition.

King Kamehameha IV

When a treaty was submitted to the United States for approval, it was rejected.

In 1863, with Kamehameha V on the throne, the Hawaiian government again sought a reciprocity treaty. It was U.S. Secretary of State Seward, who, when considering the issue, made a fateful link between reciprocity and Pearl Harbor, recommending that "...if a reciprocity treaty at any time be made with this Government, a fee simple to a piece of land at this port, sufficient for a wharf and buildings for a naval depot and also a dry dock, should be made one of the conditions of said treaty." Although reciprocity was again rejected, the link to port facilities had been clearly identified as a future bargaining tool.

By the 1870s, pressure was again building for a reciprocity treaty, most prominently from the sugar plantation owners. Real profitability and expansion required steady access to the American market.

Opposition to reciprocity had crystallized in the form of Hawaiian

King Kalākaua

King Kamehameha V

Minister of Foreign Affairs Walter Murray Gibson. Later, the supporters of Queen Emma fought reciprocity as part of their 1874 campaign to elect her to the Hawaiian throne. Emma, widow of Kamehameha IV, was opposed by David Kalākaua, who also sought to rule the Kingdom, when the throne was left vacant with the death of childless King Lunalilo in 1874.

The victorious Kalākaua was urged to action by planters who approached him in a letter soon after his election as King:

"Unless relief to the plantation interests is obtained from some quarter, it is the petitioners' opinion that serious disasters will overtake them, and with their decay the remaining business of the Kingdom will not afford a revenue to the Government..."

Initially against reciprocity, Kalākaua advised his government to draft plans with that goal in mind. A treaty proposal was presented, and after slow going in Congress, where Mainland sugar interests again blocked passage, the treaty was approved in September of 1876. Nearly 20 years after first being considered, reciprocity was now a fact.

By 1886, with reciprocity making them rich, the Hawaiian government was even more financially beholden to the sugar interests than it had been in 1876. Back in Washington, opponents of reciprocity sought abrogation of the treaty, which was originally timed for seven years, with the possibility of renewal. With that time frame passed, those in favor sought to silence the opposition by making exclusive naval rights to Pearl Harbor a precondition of American renewal.

Speaking through Gibson, Kalākaua firmly stated and restated the impossibility of such an act on several occasions. Each time, his rejections were unequivocal, as Gibson reveals in a letter dated 1997:

"The views of His Majesty's Government have already been expressed in my letter...and there is nothing...to induce any modification of them, I can therefore only repeat to Your Excellency that an arrangement to grant exclu-

Uncle Sam is seen considering just how to use Pearl Harbor to best advantage in this political cartoon, circa 1900.

The USS *Charleston* at anchor. Kalākaua traveled to California on this ship, courtesy the U.S. government. He would die in San Francisco before returning home.

sive rights to the use of any Harbor in this Kingdom to the United States, or indeed any Power whatever, is one which cannot be entertained by this country no matter what the form of words in which the proposition may be placed before us...I trust that the Pearl Harbor matter will not come up again..."

But come up again it did, both in Washington and Honolulu, with an outcome that belied Gibson's strong words. Kalākaua's position was too precarious to risk alienating those who provided his government with the substantial revenues required to run the Kingdom. In 1887, the new reciprocity treaty, with a secondary convention securing Pearl Harbor for exclusive use of the United States attached, was approved by the U.S. Congress and signed by the King. What had been impossible was now a *fait accompli*. In fact, it proved just one of many surrenders forced upon Kalākaua in the years that followed.

When Kalākaua died in 1891, the monarchy had been severely compromised. Queen Lili'uokalani's efforts at reasserting royal authority led to her overthrow and the downfall of the Hawaiian monarchy. Within five years Hawai'i would be annexed, America would be a world power, and Pearl Harbor would prove the truth of its worth.

A rustic fisherman's house on the shores of Pearl Harbor, circa 1915.

CHAPTER THREE
·
FROM PEARLS TO WARSHIPS

FROM PEARLS TO WARSHIPS

At first the navy did little with its reciprocity prize. The most modest facilities were built, barely making a presence and servicing only an occasional naval warship. All that would dramatically change with America's arrival on the world stage, that debut marked by the defeat of an enfeebled Spain in the Spanish-American War of 1898.

The American victory brought with it the spoils of empire, with Cuba and the Philippines now under the American flag. With the Indian Wars fought and won, and the country sprawling from the Atlantic to the Pacific, America was ready to move beyond its continental borders.

Possession of the Philippines meant easy access to Asia, and that reality gave new and immediate importance to Pearl Harbor as a forward base for America's expanding sphere of influence.

What had been a modest refueling station into the first years of the 20th century

Construction begins on naval facilities in 1902 (below). A decade later work is underway on dry-dock facilities (left).

would, in the span of the next four decades, evolve into a world-class naval base. Year by year facilities were added, expanding into a complex of shipyards, dry-docks, berthing areas, hangars and airfields for land-only and amphibious planes, a submarine base, plus the large resident population and accompanying facilities that made Pearl Harbor a self-contained community.

By the 1930s, with Japan in a drive for conquest, increasing numbers of military craft were at anchor in Pearl's waters. The harbor was eventually dredged to deepen its waters, but even with that accomplished it was, at deepest, a shallow 40 feet. But because of its sheltered waters and expansive size, many considered it the best natural harbor in the Pacific Islands.

As the naval port grew, Ford Island, a large flat rectangle of land in the middle of Pearl's East Loch, became a key part of the installation. Battleship Row, along Ford

Ships of the American Navy on maneuvers off Diamond Head, circa 1925. America's growing role in the Pacific and Asia made Pearl Harbor an invaluable asset. A coaling station (top) to resupply coal-powered ships, was one of the first facilities built. An article tells of a *kahuna's* efforts to assure the military success in work underway at Pearl Harbor.

Island's east coast, provided berthing facilities for the giants of the Pacific Fleet. Light carriers, destroyers, mine layers and auxiliary vessels were at anchor elsewhere along the Ford Island coast.

Pearl Harbor clearly defined Hawai'i's importance to America. Having renounced treaty limitations to their navy in 1936, Japan moved quickly to reach parity with the United States. By 1940, this had been accomplished. While the United States Navy was still slightly larger, with more than half its forces patrolling the Atlantic, Japan's military strength outstripped that of the U.S. in the Pacific. The differential ballooned after 1940, when the U.S. transferred about one-third of its Pacific Fleet to serve in the Atlantic Fleet's build-up against Nazi Germany.

In order to close the gap with a bellicose Japan, the U.S. Congress committed funds to increasing the size of the Navy by one-third by 1944. Knowing it could not match the scope of the planned U.S. buildup created a sense of urgency in Japan, where the military leadership had determined that it would be best to act quickly, while the numbers still read in Japan's favor.

As the headquarters for the U.S. Pacific Fleet after 1940, Pearl Harbor remained a well-stocked arsenal even without the major expansion that was planned. It was home base to three aircraft carriers, nine battleships, 21 cruisers, 53 destroyers and 23

Uncle Sam rolls up his sleeves to get to work at expanding Pearl's military facilities. More than $10,000,000 was appropriated by Congress for Pearl Harbor in the early 1900s. A growing number of ships made port calls by 1910, when this picture of Ford Island was taken.

submarines, plus hundreds of fighter planes and seaplanes, hospital ships, and a range of other support vessels.

The U.S. military had also established other bases on the island of O'ahu. Just to the east of Pearl Harbor was Hickam Field. Inland, on the flatland valley that separates the Ko'olau and Wai'anae volcanoes, was Wheeler Field, with additional facilities along the island's periphery manned by the Army, Navy and Marines. It was a concentration of power that made O'ahu seem invulnerable on the one hand, or a prime target on the other. The likely enemy would be Japan.

America's interests in Asia had already drawn it into confrontations with Japan. Forced to open its ports to trade by American Admiral Matthew Perry in 1854, Japan had suffered what it considered a humiliation at the hands of the Americans. Quickly adapting to changed circumstances, however, and seeing in them the seeds of opportunity, Japan had modernized, creating an impressive industrial base. Japan's parallel effort at territorial expansion and military parity with the world's leading powers set her on a collision course with the United States. ■

The build-up is obvious in this view from the early 1920s (above), with the U.S. Naval Hospital completed in 1921 (inset). A sailor strums an 'ukulele on this vintage sheet music cover, circa 1915 (left). The military presence on O'ahu mushroomed as America's power in the world grew.

A peaceful dusk descends on Pearl Harbor in a view from 'Aiea Heights, circa 1935 (above). A 1930s view of Ford Island (inset.) Sheet music cover, circa 1925 (right).

The mighty *Akagi,* flagship aircraft carrier of Japan's Combined Fleet, is backed by well-armed battleships. The aircraft carrier replaced the battleship as the key naval weapon in Japan's pursuit of empire. Painting by Tom Freeman.

CHAPTER FOUR
·
IN PURSUIT OF EMPIRE

Japanese officers on horseback during the Japanese invasion of China in 1937. Steely determination and a fanatic commitment to the Emperor and nation made dangerous enemies of the Japanese armed forces.

IN PURSUIT OF EMPIRE

International power politics and colonial ambitions would again place Hawai'i center stage. This time it would be Japan that would provide the challenge. That once-reclusive nation, unwillingly forced into opening its doors to trade by the United States in 1854, had quickly grasped the still-emerging opportunities of the industrial age. By the 1890s Japan had created an impressive industrial base, with a military machine on a par with Europe and America. Maintaining that power meant autonomy from those controlling the supply of natural resources that fueled the industrial economy. It was a need that would turn Japan into an aggressor on the international stage.

A newcomer to the international political order, Japan set out to create an empire that would provide the respect her ancient traditions deserved, and the industrial prosperity she sought to preserve.

China, weakened by civil war, was the first to feel the thrust of Japanese power. Defeated by a Japanese invasion force in 1895, China had been forced to surrender Korea and the island of Taiwan. The Japanese were further emboldened a decade later, by their defeat of the Russians in the Russo-Japanese War. From this victory Japan was ceded islands to the north of Hokkaido. Each new conquest was a stepping stone to the resource-rich lands to the west and the south.

Following World War I, the Japanese empire had once again expanded. As one of the victorious Allied Powers, Japan had been rewarded with Germany's colonial enclaves

The Japanese warship *Asama* paid a friendly visit to Hawai'i in 1925.

along the Chinese coast. Seeking more, Japan had gone on to seize parts of Germany's Pacific Island empire, taking over the Mariana, Caroline and Marshall Islands.

Poor in natural resources, Japan's strategy sought to assure a supply of necessary raw materials for industry and war in an area called the Southern Resource Area (SRA) that would make Japan the dominant power in Asia. That the SRA included lands long-claimed by others, including the Dutch East Indies (now Indonesia), British Burma, French Indochina (now Laos, Cambodia and Vietnam), and the Chinese Island of Hainan, was an unfortunate reality that made conflict inevitable.

Furthermore, Japanese interests extended beyond the SRA to include large portions of China, Taiwan, the islands of the western Pacific, and the Philippines. In some scenarios, Hawai'i was also part of the equation, potentially an eastern border to what Japan was envisioning. The Japanese called this self-defined sphere of influence the Great East Asia Co-Prosperity Sphere. By the late 1930s, establishing this protectorate became the focus of Japan's foreign policy. This required a colonial infrastructure that would allow it to develop free of foreign coercion and intervention were restricting the import of oil, steel and other industrial necessities.

Convinced that history and divine right were on its side and that it could prevail despite the risks it was provoking, Japan proved brutal in conquest and unrelenting in its drive for equity as a leading world power. The government's aggressive policies, however, set Japan on a collision course with those who sought to maintain the status quo.

Plans to upgrade and modernize the military had been underway since before the Russo-Japanese War. In the 1920s Japan was a signatory to an international convention seeking to diffuse tensions by limiting the naval strength of the great powers. And thus eliminate the threat of a ruinous arms race. The convention limited Japan's naval expansion, establishing a 5:5:3 ratio in relation to the navies of Great Britain and the United States.

By the 1930s, the treaty was in direct conflict with Japan's military objectives. Renouncing the treaty in 1936, the government quickly built its navy to a level equal to its key rivals for primacy in the Pacific. Putting its enhanced military might to work, Japan began its pursuit of empire with the conquest of Manchuria in 1931. After a brutal assault that previewed the horrors of Japanese conquest in Asia, they placed the dethroned Chinese Emperor Pu Yi on the throne of the puppet state of Manchukuo. Manchuria proved a prelude to the invasion of China in 1937, a milestone in the savagery of war. By mid-1941, the large Chinese island of Hainan had been added to Japan's China co-quests.

The United States, long committed to China's independence as a means of containing Britain, now had a new adversary in mind. It responded to Japan's aggressions by transferring its Pacific Fleet to Pearl Harbor, which became its new home port. That action and the resulting infrastructure expansion it generated were cause for concern in Tokyo and were seen as a potential threat to its imperial ambitions.

Like the concept of Manifest Destiny, which empowered America's trans-conti-

Diplomatic efforts, in part a cover for a coordinated series of attacks planned in the Pacific and South Asia, continued in Washington between U.S. Secretary of State Cordell Hull and Japanese envoys Ambassador Nomura (l) and Saburo Kurusu (r). Neither was aware of war plans already set in motion. The attack on Pearl Harbor was timed to follow delivery of a note declaring a state of war with the U.S. Delays in relaying that message meant that the attack came as a complete surprise, leaving no time for a coordinated response.

nental growth during the 19th century, the Greater East Asia Co-Prosperity Sphere proclaimed that need conferred a sanctified right to expand, even at the expense of others.

Having broken the Japanese military code, called Code Purple (MAGIC) in 1941, the United States was in a position to monitor Japanese intentions, and in September of 1940, the U.S. government warned Japan against an anticipated action against French Indochina. Two weeks later Japan signed the Tripartite Pact, allying itself with Nazi Germany and Italy.

By January of 1941 diplomatic efforts were at an impasse. While negotiations continued in Washington between Japanese Ambassador Kichisaburo Nomura and American Secretary of State Cordell Hull, the appraisal of both sides grew increasingly pessimistic.

"Japan…is on the warpath," Grew, America's Ambassador to Japan, wrote in his diary on January 1.

"A conflict with the United States…is inevitable," wrote Admiral Isoroku Yamamoto in a letter to Rear Admiral Takijiru Oikawa six days later. Both were to be proven right by events in the not-too-distant future, when Yamamoto was named Commander in Chief of the Combined Fleet, the Japanese Navy's highest command.

Although Yamamoto had not wanted to go to war with the U.S., once the Imperial Government set that course, he played an active role in planning an effective naval strategy that would include a surprise attack on Pearl Harbor.

First word of such an attack had begun to circulate as early as January, 1941, when the Peruvian Ambassador to Japan reported hearing of plans for just such a scenario to Ambassador Grew. Although Grew immediately reported the news to

Washington, he was met with skepticism by military intelligence.

In Tokyo, Foreign Minister Yosuke Matsuoka declared control of the western Pacific a non-negotiable requirement for Japan, warning that unless the United States accepts that fact, then war is inevitable.

In Washington, Secretary Knox wired Husband Kimmel, newly appointed Commander-in-Chief of the Pacific Fleet, warning him that hostilities with Japan will likely begin with a surprise attack on Pearl Harbor, further warning Kimmel to " …increase the joint readiness of the army and navy to withstand a raid." Kimmel would later claim that the government failed to provide adequate resources to adequately upgrade Pearl Harbor's defenses.

In January 1941, Japan began planning the specifics of just such an attack. By February the objectives had been defined: It was to be a surprise attack, with U.S. aircraft carriers the main target. The attack on Pearl Harbor would be followed by coordinated attacks on British Singapore and Malaya, the Philippines and other targets in Asia and the western Pacific. By first disabling American aircraft carriers and war fleet, Japan could secure its advance into south Asia and the Pacific without opposition.

As negotiations in Washington stall, the plan for Pearl Harbor is put on fast-forward in order to assure the element of surprise. In April, military intelligence in Washington alerted district commanders to the fact that the Axis partners often attacked on weekends or national holidays. Ten days later the Imperial Japanese Navy was reorganized as the First Air Fleet. In discussing the situation with President Franklin Roosevelt, General of the

The Pearl Harbor Attack Force encountered rough seas on route to Hawai'i.

Army George Marshall declared that the Japanese "…wouldn't dare attack Hawaii." Both MacArthur and Roosevelt felt the threat from Germany more pressing. As a result a portion of the Pearl Harbor-based Pacific Fleet was shifted to the Atlantic to prepare for war in Europe.

In June of 1941, the Japanese alliance with the Germans paid its first dividend when Vichy France allowed Japan to occupy French Indochina, a key Japanese objective. The U.S. retaliates by putting an embargo on oil sales to Japan, freezing Japanese assets, and closes its ports to Japanese vessels. In July a new military government, with General Hideki Tojo as Prime Minister was formed.

By November Admiral Yamamoto had detailed final plans for an attack on Pearl Harbor, as last minute negotiations took place in Washington. If negotiations had not succeeded by November 23, the countdown on an attack on Pearl Harbor is to be set in motion. The weather-linked code for such an outcome was to be 'east wind, rain.'

At the insistence of Yamamoto and Emperor Hirohito, the attack was to follow a declaration of war by 30 minutes. Failed communications voided even that limited time to respond. With the Pearl Harbor Special Attack Force already en route, Emperor Hirohito approved Yamamoto's plan of attack on the first of December, just six days before the fury of his forces would unleash four years of war. ∎

The 4,000 miles of open ocean separating Japan and Hawai'i meant that aircraft carriers had to be refueled at sea, a risky operation in the choppy waters that were encountered. In addition to six aircraft carriers with a fleet of 493 war-planes, the Special Attack Force consisted of eight destroyers, three battleships, two light cruisers, and three sub-marines. Fifteen additional submarines, several fitted with Midget subs, made their way separately to Hawai'i.

Japanese pilots below decks aboard the aircraft carrier *Akagi* en route to Pearl Harbor. The lighthearted mood was followed by on-deck lessons in the strategy of the attack. The pilots and sailors were not told of their destination until after the fleet was en route to Pearl Harbor.

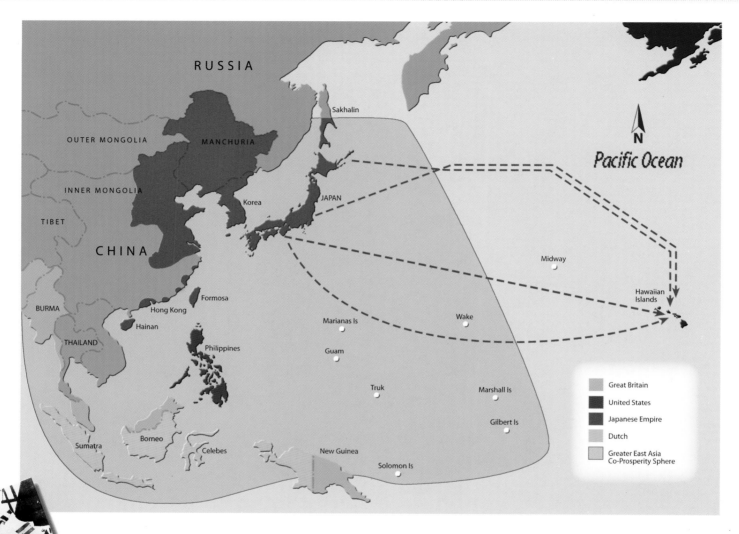

Battle-ready, the Pearl Harbor Force reached designated waters 230 miles north of O'ahu in the early morning hours of December 7 (inset). By 1941, Japan had established an empire that included the Marshall, Caroline and Mariana islands, Korea, Manchuria, French Indochina, Taiwan and parts of China. Japan now sought further expansion, including a vast area of east and south Asia that could provide Japanese industry with the raw materials it needed to prosper and pursue its ambitious military goals. Called the Greater East Asia Co-Prosperity Sphere, it was an area that included the Philippines under American administration, parts of east Asia under British control, and the Dutch East Indies—today Indonesia. Pursuit of these colonies made war with the U.S., Great Britain and the Netherlands inevitable. The surprise attack on Pearl Harbor was part of a coordinated attack plan aimed at key facilities within the Greater East Asia Co-Prosperity Sphere. Midway Island was hit the same day, with British Malaya and Singapore attacked on December 8, the Gilbert Islands on December 9—the same day Bangkok fell to the Japanese. On December 13, Japanese troops attacked the Philippines, followed a day later by the capture of Hong Kong. New Guinea was attacked on December 17. The Special Attack Force departed Hokkaido's waters on November 26, taking a northern route that skirted Alaska's Kurile Islands to avoid detection. Most of the submarine fleet had departed Japan two weeks earlier taking four different routes undetected, linking up with the Air Fleet's Special Attack Force 200 miles north of O'ahu in the early hours of December 7.

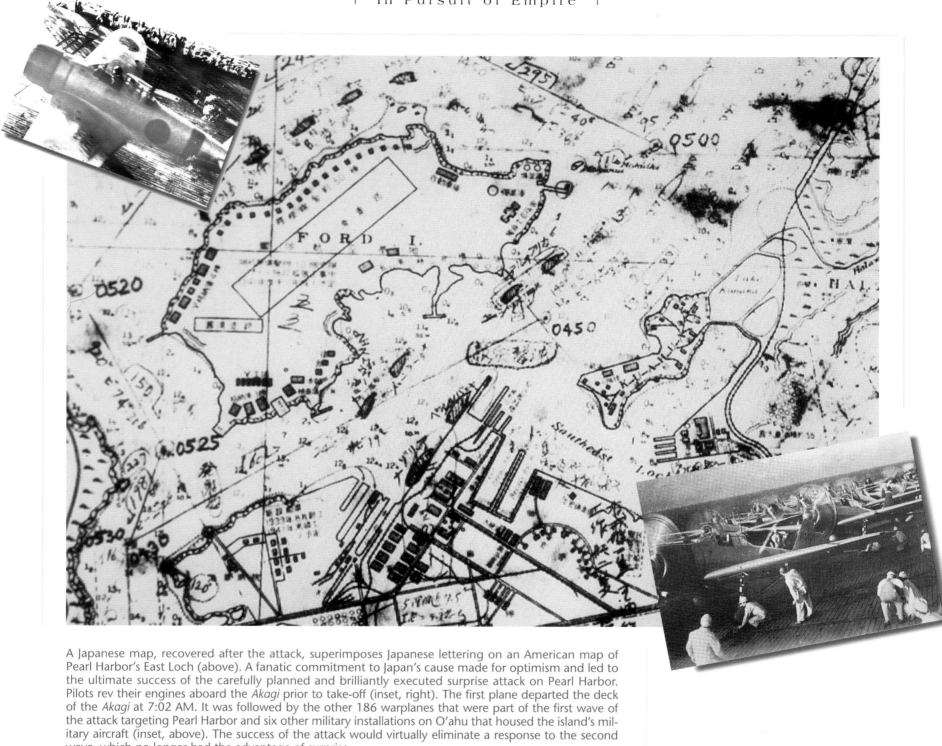

A Japanese map, recovered after the attack, superimposes Japanese lettering on an American map of Pearl Harbor's East Loch (above). A fanatic commitment to Japan's cause made for optimism and led to the ultimate success of the carefully planned and brilliantly executed surprise attack on Pearl Harbor. Pilots rev their engines aboard the *Akagi* prior to take-off (inset, right). The first plane departed the deck of the *Akagi* at 7:02 AM. It was followed by the other 186 warplanes that were part of the first wave of the attack targeting Pearl Harbor and six other military installations on O'ahu that housed the island's military aircraft (inset, above). The success of the attack would virtually eliminate a response to the second wave, which no longer had the advantage of surprise.

FORCEFUL LEADERS, CONFLICTED TIMES

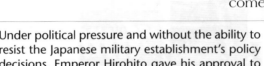

Strong leaders with an appetite for empire made a Japanese war against the United States inevitable. It was leaders of the generation coming of age as the 20th century dawned, who would seek to implement the government's plan for military conquest.

Indoctrinated with strict discipline and unchallenged loyalty to the nation and its honor, they saw the use of power as a logical expression of national policy, with national honor an ideal worthy of any personal sacrifice.

Emperor Hirohito (1901-1989)

Emperor Hirohito, who ruled from 1926 until his death in 1989, played an enigmatic role in the formation of policy throughout the crucial years leading to Pearl Harbor. While *samurai* no longer ruled through the Shogunate, the military, through its hierarchy of career officers, increasingly came to dominate in formulating policy.

While they acted in the Emperor's name, it is generally accepted that Hirohito was a figurehead, acquiescing to the decisions of his generals and admirals, in spite of what may have been personal reservations about the direction their actions were heading.

Under political pressure and without the ability to resist the Japanese military establishment's policy decisions, Emperor Hirohito gave his approval to the military's plan for the surprise attack on Pearl Harbor on December 1 (above). Admiral Isoroku Yamamoto was an ardent nationalist whose strategy was executed at Pearl Harbor (below).

Admiral Isoroku Yamamoto (1884-1943)

Graduating from naval school seventh in his class, Osoroku Yamamoto would rise to the pinnacle of power as Japan expanded its navy in the 1930s. Initially opposed to war with the United States, considering the long-term outcome problematic, it was his strategy for victory that was implemented after a policy of expansion had been established as national policy by Premier Hideki Tojo.

Having served as an ensign in the Russo-Japanese War, it was the battles of World War I that convinced him that the future of warfare lay with airplanes and aircraft carriers. Victory would go to the nation that most effectively replaced the destroyers and cruisers that were still the dominant armament of the world's great navies, with aircraft carriers and bombers.

Yamamoto was familiar with the United States, having spent time studying the petroleum industry at Harvard University, then as a military attache in Washington, D.C. It was his rejection of existing treaties limiting Japan's naval expansion that became official policy, making him a hero for having faced down Japan's future enemies: Great Britain and the United States.

Conservative, and, as it turned out, accurate, in his appraisal of Japan's ultimate ability to prevail in war and conquest, he was an ardent nationalist who

implemented a policy he considered the only way to victory. That policy meant a reliance on aircraft carriers and their aircraft to secure Japan's territorial objectives. This policy included Yamamoto's plan for a massive surprise air attack on Pearl Harbor. As Commander in Chief of the Combined Fleet he accompanied the armada that attacked Pearl Harbor.

Vice-Admiral Chuichi Nagumo, commander of the Special Attack Force (above). A grim-faced Franklin Roosevelt, with General MacArthur (l) and Husband Kimmel (below).

The victory at Pearl Harbor spoke well for Yamamoto's strategy, but America quickly rebuilt its naval power and went on the offensive. Yamamoto was killed on April 18, 1943, his plane shot down by American fighters.

Vice-Admiral Chuichi Nagumo (1887-1944)

Of a fiery temperament and aggressive nature, Nagumo rose through the ranks to become commander of the First Air Fleet. He commanded the air attack on Pearl Harbor from the deck of his flagship, the aircraft carrier *Akagi*. It was Nagumo who decided to call off a planned third air attack on Pearl Harbor, deciding that the risk of an American response was too great. Many consider this a fateful blunder in terms of the additional damage that might have been inflicted. He would ultimately loose the *Akagi* as well as three other of Japan's aircraft carriers, in battles in the Indian Ocean, the Dutch East Indies, and Midway. He com-

mitted suicide in July, 1944, once Japan's defeat was evident.

President Franklin Roosevelt (1882-1945)

Franklin Roosevelt was just at the start of his third term when events began spiraling out of control relative to Japanese designs on Asia and the Pacific's islands. The Tripartite Treaty between Japan, Germany and Italy meant that the Nazi threat in Europe would also involve fighting a Pacific front. Although possessing the world's largest navy and one of the most technologically advanced, fighting a two front war diluted U.S. power.

Realizing this President Roosevelt sought to delay the inevitable for as long as possible, providing the United States with time to upgrade its fleet in preparation for a two-front world war. By the late 1930s, however, it was obvious that negotiations were not going to set things straight. That realization saw Congress appropriate funds for a 30% increase in the size of the naval fleet by 1944.

Roosevelt had made Pearl Harbor the headquarters of the U.S. Pacific Fleet in 1940 as a signal to Japan that it was risking war. Several top military advisers warned against the move, fearing Pearl Harbor's vulnerability. He was aware that this increased the possibility of a surprise attack, but decided this forward projection of American power was a necessary deterrent in the impending confrontation with Japan. Roosevelt

War was imminent when General of Short (l) and Commander in Chief of Kimmel (r) escorted Britain's Lord

the Army, Hawaiian department, Walter C. the U.S. Pacific Fleet, Admiral Husband E. Mountbatten on a visit to Pearl Harbor.

played an active policy role in plotting military strategy with his chiefs-of-staff. A realist of Churchillian certainty and charisma, there are those who say he failed to act on advance information about a planned Japanese attack on Pearl Harbor in hopes of drawing America into the war already being fought in Europe. This scenario remains unconfirmed, although preoccupations with Europe, no doubt, made for some serious miscalculations as to what was to unfold in Asia and the Pacific. In fact, Japan's move against the United States was audacious enough to be considered no more than a slight possibility, although the potential for an attack had been widely discussed at the highest levels of government from the late '30s on.

Admiral Husband E. Kimmel (1882-1968)

Pearl Harbor's naval forces were under the command of Admiral Husband E. Kimmel on the morning of December 7. Well-respected, with a careful, reasonable nature, Kimmel had graduated from Annapolis in 1904. In 1931 he had been selected over 32 other officers as Commander in Chief Pacific. When he took command at Pearl Harbor he was the Navy's senior admiral. At Pearl Harbor, Kimmel was confronted with a command problem that he felt placed the facility at risk. Responsibility for the facility was split between the Army and the Navy, with the Army responsible for the vital land and air defenses that protected the entire installation, although the navy was

responsible for the Navy Yard. And while the Navy was responsible for reconnaissance, it was the Army that controlled the radar stations and air and shore defenses in case of an invasion. Kimmel also felt the U.S. focus on Europe was at the expense of Asia. Not only had ships been transferred to the Atlantic Fleet, but supplies were short and the sense of urgency alternating with a casualness that belied real concern. After the attack Kimmel was transferred from Pearl Harbor while eight separate investigations sought to pin the blame for Pearl Harbor. While Kimmel was never court-martialed, he was censured for failing to better coordinate O'ahu's defense with the Army. The same charge was lodged against the Army's commander, Major-General Walter C. Short. Kimmel retired from the military in 1942 and spent time throughout the remaining years of his life clearing his name.

Major-General Walter C. Short (1880-1949)

A training officer in France during World War 1, Walter C. Short was given command of the Army's Hawaiian Department in February of 1941. A competent commander, Short was surprised by the Japanese attack despite government warnings that such an attack was a definite possibility. Ten days after the attack he was replaced by General Emmons. The investigations of the Pearl Harbor attack found him derelict in directing his staff and uncooperative in his dealings with the Navy. Retiring from the military in 1942, he died while still seeking to clear his name, claiming that Washington had failed to provide adequate information on what was brewing. Echoing Kimmel's defense, he

Admiral Chester Nimitz was named on December 31, 1941, replacing Harbor and the Pacific fleet and led the until the end of the war.

Commander in Chief of the U.S. Pacific Fleet Kimmel. He oversaw the restoration of Pearl Navy's brilliant battle plan for the Pacific

Pilots of the attack fleet pose on the deck of the *Akagi* en route to Pearl Harbor (left). They were guided by a fanatic dedication to the Emperor and Japan's national honor. American servicemen during the salvage effort that followed the attack on Pearl Harbor (right).

claimed the government had failed to provide the resources required to maintain Pearl Harbor as a significant deterrent and assure a proper defense in case of attack. In fact Pearl Harbor's defenses were inadequate, without the necessary anti-aircraft guns or fighter defenses to repel an attack, even with ample warning.

Opposing Forces

By 1940, Japanese forces, most particularly the navy, were on a par for firepower and capability with their American counterparts. Both the United States and Japan had upgraded their forces in the decades following World War I. New technologies were quickly making old defenses and delivery systems obsolete. The battleship, long the naval standard of power, for example, was being forced into a support position by the aircraft carrier and its resident planes. Submarines were also now a standard component of naval warfare.

In total numbers the U.S. had a larger navy and air force than did Japan, but with a war in the Atlantic and the Pacific to fight simultaneously, the advantage was on the side of Japan. A comparison between the American and Japanese forces reveals a disparity in the Pacific that led Japan to act as quickly and surreptitiously as possible.

While the United States had three aircraft carriers in its Pacific Fleet, Japan had 10. The battleship count listed nine for the U.S., twelve for Japan. As for cruisers, it was 21 for the U.S. and 35 for Japan. With 110 destroyers, Japan had more than double the U.S. count of 53, including many ships of first-world-war vintage. With an expansion of the American Fleet imminent, the Japanese decided to act while the numbers were still in their favor.

As November of 1941 drew to a close a select number of ships, including Japan's six largest aircraft carriers and an armada of escort vessels assembled in the waters off the northern island of Hokkaido. Secrecy was crucial, and only those in the topmost chain of command knew what was about to happen. It would not be long, however, before the world would find out just what Imperial Japan had in mind.

An impressive portion of Japan's Combined Fleet, with Mt. Fuji in the distance (left). A portion of the powerful U.S. Pacific Fleet in Pearl Harbor's waters, with the Wai'anae Mountains as a backdrop (right).

The tanker *Neosho* backs away from Ford Island to avoid Japanese planes. A burning Val fighter tries to gain altitude. The Japanese lost nine fighters, 15 dive-bombers, and five torpedo bombers in the attack. In comparison, the U.S. lost 161 planes, almost all on the ground.

CHAPTER FIVE

WAR COMES TO PARADISE
December 7, 1941

The last days of peace. Two views of Pearl Harbor in late 1941, one looking toward the Ko'olau Mountains, the other focused on Ford Island and the harbor's East Loch.

WAR COMES TO PARADISE
DECEMBER 7, 1941

Departing Hokkaido on November 26, the main fleet of the Pearl Harbor Attack Force plotted a course through the frigid waters off Alaska's Kurile Islands. The route passed through lightly trafficked waters, thus limiting the possibility of detection. Secrecy, rigidly maintained while the attack was planned, was equally critical in the transfer of the Attack Force to the distant battleground. As cover to the departure of a significant portion of the fleet, naval bases issued false shore leaves to cover for missing personnel, while shore stations faked ship-to-shore radio traffic in an effort to deceive those eavesdropping.

Luckily for the Japanese, no other ships were spotted throughout the eleven-day-long journey from Hokkaido to the sub-tropic waters 200 miles north of O'ahu chosen as base for the Attack Force.

The Pearl Harbor Attack Force was a well-integrated fighting machine. It included six aircraft carriers, led by the 848-foot *Akagi*, flagship of the fleet. The

A Japanese Kate torpedo bomber, the most lethal weapon used in the attack, over Hickam Field. Each squadron of planes had a carefully planned attack route.

carriers carried more than 400 planes, a mix of Val dive-bombers, Zero fighters, and Kate high-level and torpedo bombers equipped to release a combination of low-level torpedoes and high-altitude bombs. Additional relief planes were stored below the main deck.

Three massive air attacks were planned, with Pearl Harbor the primary objective. But the attacks also took careful aim at other military installations on O'ahu, including Wheeler Field, the main Army Air Force fighter base; Kāne'ohe Naval Air Station, home to O'ahu's key long-range reconnaissance fleet; Bellows Field, an Army Air Force auxiliary base; Hickam Air Field, adjacent to Pearl Harbor and home to the army's main bomber squads; and 'Ewa Marine Air Station, where 47 planes were based. All would suffer major damage, thus limiting the opportunity for American planes to take to the air and respond.

The first Japanese warplanes left the flat-top deck of the *Akagi* with an estimat-

Ford Island, November 1941. Battle ship row is at bottom right. The aircraft carrier *Lexington* is at anchor to the upper left. None of the Pacific Fleet's three aircraft carriers were in port at the time of the attack. It would prove a bit of fateful timing, allowing the U.S. to implement a battle plan for the Pacific that led to Japan's ultimate defeat. A Japanese pilot's attack map clearly identifies potential targets (inset).

A plume of smoke over Hickam Field identifies a first wave strike success. Hickam would be a prime target of the second wave as well (inset). The faint ripple in the foreground identifies a torpedo's underwater progress leading to a direct hit against the *West Virginia* and the *Oklahoma* in these Japanese photos of the first phase of the attack (above).

Hit by gunfire after dropping its 1,750-pound torpedo, a Kate torpedo bomber, its pilot dead, falls toward the seaplane tender *Curtiss*. After the plane struck it, the *Curtiss* exploded in a ball of flames. Badly damaged, the *Curtiss* was repaired and restored to service in May of 1942.

ed time of arrival over Pearl Harbor at 7:45 AM. Skies were clear, seas calm, but flying time proved longer than expected, with the first attack clocked to 7:52 A.M. at Wheeler Airfield. Within minutes, warplanes had hit the 'Ewa Marine Air Station and Ford Island. Attack leader Mitsuo Fujita radioed the good news: "Tora,"—meaning surprise achieved.

Well-trained and fearless, almost courting death in fulfilling their obligations to the Emperor and the nation, the pilots of the Imperial Navy's air fleet would brilliantly implement Yamamoto's attack strategy, revealed to them only after the attack force was underway.

The attack was designed for the sleepy early hours of Sunday morning. Spies on O'ahu, positioned with the Japanese consulate in Honolulu were surprised to find it quite easy to monitor events in the harbor from upcountry lookouts open to all. In assessing blame, failure to understand the threat as imminent was the underlying cause of Pearl Harbor's vulnerability. It would prove a costly miscalculation.

Coming in from the north, the first wave of Japanese planes was identified on radar screens while still over the ocean. The sightings were ignored at headquarters, however, thought to be a group of American planes scheduled to arrive from California that day. With that early warning opportunity lost, the Japanese planes had virtually unimpeded access to O'ahu's skies, raining devastating blows on all of the military's key installations.

As it turned out, the Pacific Fleet's three aircraft carriers, the stated objective of the attack, were not in port on the morning of the attack. In this the U.S. forces were lucky. In terms of battleships, however, it was something of a full house, with eight of the nine

The magazine of the destroyer *Shaw* explodes after a direct hit. By 10 AM, with the last of the Japanese planes departed, ships in the waters around Ford Island are ablaze, as are drydock facilities, Ford Island Naval Air Station and Hickam Field Army Air Base.

in the Pacific Fleet at anchor when the attack began, defensively clustered near Ford Island to protect against sabotage. The same rationale saw the military's planes clustered on airfield runways, making them easy targets.

The first wave of warplanes reached Pearl Harbor at 7:35 A.M., inflicting massive destruction on all facilities attacked. The element of surprise had been an unequivocal success. It was followed by an equally devastating series of attacks that began when the second wave of 167 planes attacked at 8:40 A.M. Luckily, none carried aerial torpedoes, or the results might have been even more devastating.

By 10 A.M. it was all over. In two and a half hours the Pacific Fleet had been significantly reduced in capability. Smoke rose in great plumes, ink-black clouds hiding the landscape. Flames rose in great explosive swirls as fuel and munitions were ignited. As sirens wailed, Pearl Harbor entered the annals of history. ∎

The attack, as seen from 'Aiea Heights. Smoke billows from the ships off Ford Island and over Hickam Field (above). The flag still flies from the bow of the stricken *West Virginia* (inset).

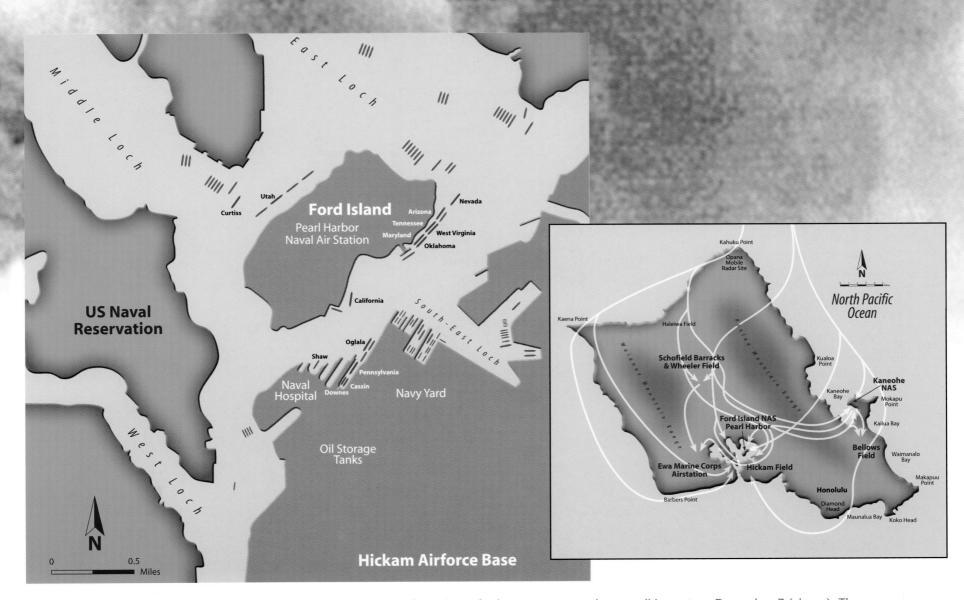

Map with Ford Island Battleships, destroyers, cruisers and a variety of other support vessels were all in port on December 7 (above). The Pacific Fleet's three aircraft carriers, the primary targets of the attack, however, were all out of port and thus survived the attack unscathed. In addition to the ships that were damaged or destroyed, planes were also destroyed on the ground at Pearl Harbor Naval Air Station on Ford Island, and at the Army's Hickam Airfield, just to the east of Pearl Harbor. In addition to Pearl Harbor Naval Air Station and Hickam, the attack included four other military installations on O'ahu. The intricate and carefully choreographed attack launched in two consecutive waves of fighters—high altitude bombers and torpedo bombers (inset). The First Wave attack began at 7:35 A.M (arrows from left). The Second Wave began at 8:40 A.M. and ended at 10 A.M., when all planes returned to the Special Attack Force, positioned 200 miles to the north of Pearl Harbor (arrows from right).

The harbor ablaze, seen from Pearl's east shore (above). The *Arizona* lies sunk and burning several hours after the attack (inset).

Hickam Field is in flames after a 90-minute-long series of attacks (inset). Hit several times by torpedoes and bombs during the second wave of the attack, the battleship *Nevada* sought to escape (above). Her commander, fearful she would be sunk and block the harbor entrance, purposely beached the *Nevada* to avoid that possibility.

Clouds of smoke darken the skies over Battleship Row (above). The tender *Oglala* is capsized, while the *Shaw* burns in the distance (inset).

Hangar #1 on Ford Island is hit (above). Twenty-six planes were lost. Facilities at the Army's Wheeler Field are ablaze. Fifty-three planes were lost at Wheeler (inset).

Caught off-guard, the successful attacks against military aircraft during the first wave made a significant aerial response impossible (above). Only a handful of planes made it airborne, and most of these were shot down in the attempt to gain altitude. Several took to the air in time for the second wave, downing several Japanese warplanes. In total 164 planes were destroyed, with another 159 damaged. The Marines, Army and Navy all lost aircraft at the six military installations that were hit on December 7. Salvage efforts at Kāne'ohe Naval Air Station began even as the attack was underway (inset).

Watching the attack from a Honolulu street corner. At first many thought they were war games. It quickly proved more serious, with more than 40 civilian casualties and property damage the result of misdirected bombs and failed anti-aircraft fire.

"Yesterday, December 7, 1941—a date which shall live in infamy—the United States of America was suddenly and deliberately attacked by naval and air forces of the Empire of Japan..."

Moored next to each other on Battleship Row, the *West Virginia* and the *Tennessee* were repeatedly hit by Japanese aircraft. The *West Virginia,* hit by between five and seven torpedoes and two bombs, sunk. Both ships were eventually repaired and returned to service.

President Franklin Roosevelt addresses Congress on December 8, and war is declared against Japan.

A Japanese postcard, one of a series issued on the first anniversary of the attack (above). News of the attack made Pearl Harbor a familiar name around the world: *Honolulu Star-Bulletin*, The *San Francisco Examiner*, The *New York Times* and *Le Figaro* (Paris) (insets).

WAR EXTRA
WAR DECLARED
U.S. FLEET SAILS
BATTLESHIP BOMBED
2ND RAID ON HONOLULU
2ND SUNDAY EXTRA

VÖLKISCHER BEOBACHTER
Die ersten harten Schläge sind gefallen
Japans Waffen antworten Roosevelt
Der Kriegshetzer muß schon schwere Verluste der USA.-Flotte auf Hawai zugeben
Hawai und Singapur bombardiert

The Sydney Morning Herald

Shriners Stage Colorful Grid Show
The Honolulu Advertiser
F. D. R. WILL SEND MESSAGE
TO EMPEROR ON WAR CRISIS
14 Bands Play In Spectacular Benefit Affair

Volkischer Beobachter (Berlin), *Sydney Morning Herald* and *The Honolulu Advertiser.*

TORPEDO WARFARE, FIGHTER BOMBERS, SUBMARINES & MIDGET SUBS

Pearl Harbor provided the Japanese armed forces with some very specific challenges beyond the element of surprise. Foremost were Pearl Harbor's shallow waters, for the torpedo attacks that were a key element of Japanese strategy required 300-foot depth to operate effectively.

To be successful in Pearl Harbor's 40-foot-depths required adaptations to both aerial and submarine-launched torpedoes. Modified with fins, they proved their effectiveness in a devastating series of direct hits that immobilized the battleships of the Pacific Fleet.

The first wave attack planes were configured to wreak as much havoc as possible, making the most of the element of surprise. There were 40 Kate torpedo bombers, each equipped with one 1,750-pound air torpedo. There were also 49 Kate high-altitude bombers, each carrying 1,750-pound, armor-piercing bombs.

Then there were 43 Zero fighters, accompanying the bombers to prevent interference from any American planes that might make it into the air. The suddenness of the attack and its comprehensive selection of targets meant almost none did. With little opposition, the Zeros proved their destructive worth in the attacks on O'ahu's air bases, high-power strafing setting planes afire and killing those in their line of fire.

The modified torpedoes proved accurate and deadly, severely damaging eight battleships, plus a number of cruisers, destroyers and other naval vessels anchored in and around Ford Island. Of the 40 aerial torpedoes carried into attack, more than 30 hit targets, with many ships shattered by multiple hits. Aerial torpedoes accounted for 40 percent of the hits, including some of the most devastating, sharing the honors for destructive impact with the armor-piercing bombs dropped from as high as 6,000 feet. Two depth charges would add to the carnage.

Having no advance certainty that its planes would be able to breach American defenses with its air force, the Pearl Harbor Attack Force included a large submarine division. Divided into four squadrons, the Special Attack Force departed Japanese waters on November 11, more than two weeks earlier than the main Air Attack Force. Designed for a backup role in the main attack plan, they would prove its least successful component.

The fleet included five specially fitted

Kate bomber releases a deadly torpedo. Modified for Pearl Harbor's shallow waters, the torpedo bombers proved an especially effective weapon in the attack's success (above). Midget subs in drydock (below). Nearly 80 feet long, they were only six feet at their widest, providing cramped quarters for the two-man crew. Each was equipped with two torpedoes, none of which hit its target.

submarines, each of which carried a two-man midget sub. Developed in the 1930s, the midget subs were designed to be carried to combat positions piggy-backed to a 358-foot mother sub. Just under 80-feet long and six feet at their widest, they proved claustrophobic confinement and proved ineffectual in the attack. The plan called for them to enter Pearl Harbor, protected by large subs positioned along the coast. When the attack began, they were to join in, attacking ships as they circumnavigated Ford Island. Of all the elements of the attack, the midget subs proved the most disappointing in implementation. One, its gyro-compass broken, lost its way and headed east, eventually beaching itself on the reef off Bellows Field in Kāne'ohe. Of the two-man crew, one died, and the other became America's first Japanese prisoner of war. Only one midget penetrated the harbor, and it was sunk after two failed torpedo firings. Three were sunk by a depth charges in the waters out-

A midget sub is salvaged from Pearl Harbor's waters (above left). Its gyroscope broken, one of the midget subs got lost and ended up beached on Kāne'ohe's sandy shores (above, right). A painting honors nine of the 10 midget submariners who took part in the attack, pictured in the central image (below). All died in the attack. The 10th was captured, considered a dishonor, and therefore he has not been included in the painting. While Yamamoto's overall strategy was very successful, the use of midget subs proved an ill-fated aspect of the attack.

side the harbor.

The submarines were not expected to operate in the shallow confines of Pearl Harbor, but should any vessel escape or be found at sea, they were vulnerable to the sub's 20 torpedoes. As a component of the Pearl Harbor Attack Force they were designed for reconnaissance and to intercept counterattacks against Nagumo's carrier fleet. The submarine fleet included five specially fitted submarines, each of which carried a two-man midget sub. Developed in the 1930s, the midget subs were designed to be carried to combat positions piggy-backed to the 358-foot mother sub.

These five subs reached O'ahu on the evening of December 6. Surfacing after dark to allow the midget-sub crew to enter their long, slim minisub, crewmen on deck later reported seeing the night lights of Waikīkī in the distance.

Released from their mother subs in the early-morning hours of December 7, the plan called for them to enter Pearl Harbor underwater, await the aerial attack, and then add to the chaos with torpedo attacks of their own.

The USS *Arizona* in Pearl Harbor's calm waters. Launched in 1918 and substantially upgraded and modernized twice in the 1930s, the USS *Arizona* was a state-of-the-art warship (inset). The Pacific Fleet in battle lineup, headed by the *Arizona*.

CHAPTER SIX
·
THE USS *ARIZONA*

The newly launched *Arizona* sails out of New York harbor on its 1918 inaugural run. Too late for a World War I assignment, she served as a training ship with the Atlantic Fleet until being transferred to the Pacific Fleet.

THE USS ARIZONA

Like the galleons of the Spanish Armada, the China Clippers of tradeship days, the ironclad *Monitor* and *Merrimac* of Civil War fame, and the *Titanic* and *Lusitania,* the battleship *Arizona* was destined to become a symbol of iconic significance—despite the fact that she never fired a shot in wartime service. The story starts in another era, fast fading to memory even as the *Arizona* was being commissioned.

Work was started on the USS *Arizona* in 1914, and was completed in October, 1917, six months after the United States entered World War I. Steaming out of New York Harbor on her maiden voyage, she joined the Atlantic Fleet, where she served as a gunnery training ship. Following the armistice of November 1918, she sailed with the British Grand Fleet, after which she was transferred to San Pedro, California, where she was attached to the growing Pacific Fleet.

Designed to match advances in warship design triggered by Japan's emergence as a world-class naval power, the *Arizona* was one of the most powerful battleships of her day. With an overall length of 608 feet and a crew of more than 1,700, she was one of two Pennsylvania-class battleships commissioned by the U.S. Navy during the early 20th-century race for naval

Visitors pay a visit to the *Arizona* in 1925. Her big guns had a range of up to 20 miles.

supremacy between Britain, Germany, Japan and the United States.

Carrying twelve impressive 18-inch guns in four distinctive triple turrets, she could travel at 21 knots and was widely praised for her steady handling and the precision and impact of her long-range guns. Once in 1929, and again in the early 1930s, she had been dry-docked and extensively upgraded to modernize her capabilities and adapt her defenses to suit the new, more powerful weapons introduced in the years following World War I. In 1940 she was transferred to Pearl Harbor as flagship of America's Pacific Fleet. It was here that fate would provide her with a permanent home.

Although by the late 1930s the impact of air power had made aircraft carriers the delivery system of the future, the *Arizona* and her sister battleships remained key components of American naval power. Their great size, decks bristling with massive guns, inspired respect. Now that power lay shattered.

While many of the ships damaged on December 7 would be salvaged, rebuilt and sent back into service, the *Arizona* would not be one of them. She was anchored at quay F-7 of Battleship Row when the bomb-and-torpedo attack began. From her

Dry Dock Number One at Pearl Harbor was an important facility in the repair and maintenance of ships. The USS *Arizona* is shown prior to the Pearl Harbor attack undergoing repair (above). The battleship *California* in Dry Dock Number One undergoing salvage and repair as a result of the attack on December 7, 1941 (inset).

decks, sailors out to raise the Stars and Stripes saw planes approaching, and then watched dumb-struck as torpedo bombers attacked the *Oklahoma* and *West Virginia*, at anchor nearby.

Within minutes it was the *Arizona's* turn, with the first set of bombs, 1,750-pound giants, exploded astern and aft. The repair ship *Vestal*, adjacent to the *Arizona*, also took two direct hits. But it would be the next series of bombs, hitting forward, near gun turret #2, that would provide the fatal blow. Within seconds of hitting its target the 16-inch bomb had penetrated the first and second decks, stopping at the third level deep within the ship. Here it exploded, igniting the ship's forward magazine. Within seconds the ship was engulfed in smoke and flames. Torn apart by cataclysmic explosions, the *Arizona* quickly sank to her upper deck, turrets twisted like skeletal arms, giant guns collapsed into her interior. The oil fire that followed, fed by the *Arizona's* 4,600 tons of fuel, burned for two days.

About one-third of the 1,731 men aboard the *Arizona* survived.

Below decks, in the *Arizona's* modern galley. More than 1,100 men were trapped below decks when the ship suffered a series of cataclysmic explosions.

From the pictures that show the attack, their survival seems a miracle. The loss of 1,177 men—including Captain Franklin Van Valkenburgh and Rear Admiral Isaac Kidd, Commander of Battleship Division One—made this the worst single disaster in U.S. naval history. Both Van Valkenburgh and Kidd were posthumously awarded the Congressional Medal of Honor.

In salvaged parts the *Arizona* would live on. Massive guns and turrets were removed and reused. But there was no way her 32,500-ton displacement would ever again see the light of day.

Oil still leaks from the *Arizona's* sunken hull, creating expanding rainbows that slowly fade as they drift into the broad expanse of Pearl Harbor's calm waters. Of all the ships that were lost or damaged that day, none remains as alive as the *Arizona*. Like the *Titanic,* she is the symbol of profound loss. This defeat has secured her a greater place in history than any victory might have otherwise afforded. ■

The USS *Honolulu* receives a grand scale welcome at Aloha Tower on a visit in 1939 after transferring to Pearl Harbor from San Diego (above). The *Honolulu* was representative of the many cruisers that comprised the Pacific Fleet. Two years later, that fleet would be heavily damaged during the 1941 Pearl Harbor attack. Pictured is the dramatic loss of the battleship USS *Arizona* (inset).

Engulfed in smoke, the *Arizona* suffered eight direct bomb hits. The explosions that followed damaged the ship beyond repair. Here the foremast and the bridge collapse as the forward section of the ship is destroyed by the exploding magazine.

Two days of oil fires that followed the bombings left the *Arizona* a tangled mass of wreckage (above, opposite). Sunk to her upper deck, her turrets damaged or destroyed, all useable parts of the ship were salvaged in the two years that followed the attack (insets).

Black smoke obscures the burning *West Virginia,* as sailors valiantly try and put out the fires.

CHAPTER SEVEN
·
THE AFTERMATH

Sailors put leis on the graves of those lost at the Kāne'ohe Naval Air Station.

THE AFTERMATH

When the smoke cleared it was obvious that America had suffered a devastating blow. Both its naval battle fleet and its air forces in the Pacific had been decimated and thousands of lives had been lost.

Although the three aircraft carriers attached to the Pacific Fleet had escaped unscathed, eight of its nine battleships had been badly damaged, including three that were sunk. Destroyers and light cruisers were likewise damaged, as were auxiliary vessels; 164 planes were lost and 159 damaged, along with air hangars and other facilities.

Then there was the toll in human lives, with the Navy losing 1,999 sailors, the Army 233 soldiers, and the Marines 109 men. In addition, 49 civilians were killed by off-target bombs and mistimed anti-aircraft shells that fell back on the city. Dozens of buildings were damaged or destroyed.

The dead were found at home and in the streets. They were found floating in Pearl's oil-coated waters, afire for days after the attack. Others were found sprawled on Ford Island's flatlands, where bombers and fighters had inflicted considerable damage with machine-gun strafing. Altogether, 2,390 Americans would lose

Rescue efforts were underway even before the attack ended. Here a sailor is pulled from the waters off the stricken *West Virginia*.

their lives that day. Most of the bodies were never recovered, lost to a watery grave or melted into eternity by the heat of fires that raged for hours and days.

Even before the Japanese planes of the second wave had left the sky, rescue efforts were underway to save the lives of sailors trapped below decks or in waters aflame with fuel oil. Seemingly impossible rescues were accomplished that day, thanks to the bravery of those who survived the attack and a rapid response on the part of the Navy and the Army.

It was all over in two and a half hours, but the repercussion of the attack would have both short-term and long-term consequences for the United States. In fact, this was not just an attack against Pearl Harbor, but an attack on the American assumption of invincibility.

Psychologically speaking, there were two very different stages in the recovery process. The first was defined by shock, horror and vulnerability. The second was expressed with confidence, unity of purpose, and a shared commitment that was clearly focused on avenging the losses suffered on December 7.

Hit by two bombs, the *Tennessee* was only moderately damaged.
She was repaired and rejoined the Pacific Fleet.

While investigators found fault with both Kimmel's and Short's performances, it was ultimately two fatal miscalculations on the national level that led to Pearl Harbor. The first was in considering Hawai'i as inviolable, both because it was so distant from Japan and because it was an integral part of the United States. That made it too risky a target. The second miscalculation was the failure to take into account the intelligence, skill and ingenuity the Japanese brought to the battlefield.

Even here it is hard to lay blame, for the nation was still in the midst of dealing with a decade-long depression. And in Europe, a decade of compromise had simply paved the way for Nazi Germany's unchecked rise to power. The rush of events that was remaking the map was also setting up sides for another world war.

Perhaps Pearl Harbor, and all of O'ahu, should already have been on a war footing by December. It was no secret

The destroyers *Downes* (l) and *Cassin* were severely damaged while in drydock. Neither ship proved salvageable, and they were both scrapped in 1942. The more moderately damaged battleship *Pennsylvania* is behind the *Downes* and *Cassin*.

that relations between Japan and the United States were leading to war, not resolution. And although there had been numerous warnings, no one anticipated Japan's ability to pull off a raid over such distances and of such concentrated strength. It was all in the timing, a fact as true for the fate of nations as for individuals.

It did not take long for Pearl Harbor to have a positive impact on America's consciousness. The shock of unexpected events can have a catalytic impact. So it was with December 7, 1941. From fear and uncertainty came courage and resolve. By December 8, President Roosevelt was addressing a joint session of Congress, declaring the United States of America at war with Imperial Japan.

The will of the American people was steeled by Pearl Harbor. Honoring and avenging those lost became a national priority. ■

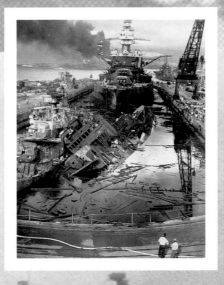

The *Cassin* and *Downes* (above, inset). At the ready, marksmen look skyward. Poorly prepared before the attack, the military immediately made providing security and anti-aircraft defenses a priority, with Hawai'i serving as America's headquarters for the war in the Pacific (right, inset). Sailors on Ford Island pensively relax awaiting a possible second attack. In the background is the beached battleship *Nevada* (above).

Sailors approach the capsized *Oklahoma* on a rescue mission (above). A serviceman pays a visit to the tangled wreckage of the refloated ship. A two-year-long repair effort raised the ship, but after a careful evaluation she was not returned to service (inset).

The *Cassin* sinks into the waters of the flooded dry dock (above).
Even a thick metal skin proves inadequate to the impact of a fast-
moving, 1,750-pound torpedo (inset).

The twisted remains of the USS *Shaw* (above) and a bomb crater aboard the *Downes* (inset).

The aircraft carrier *Shokaku*, sunk off the Philippine coast in 1944 (above). Japan was unable to sustain the momentum of victory that Pearl Harbor seemed to offer. Further, having failed to damage the Pacific Fleet's aircraft carriers, it was possible for the United States to provide Japan with an immediate challenge in battles that would be fought across the Pacific. Before the war was over, all of the aircraft carriers and many of the other ships that were part of the Pearl Harbor Attack Force had been destroyed in battle. The *Akagi*, pride of the Japanese Combined Fleet, was sunk by U.S. dive-bombers on June 4, 1942 during the Battle of Midway, as were the *Kaga,* the *Hiryu* and the *Soryu.* Other losses followed at Guadalcanal, Leyte Gulf, and the Solomon Islands. The Japanese Navy never recovered from the losses. Japanese prisoners of war are shipped to Pearl Harbor for incarceration (inset).

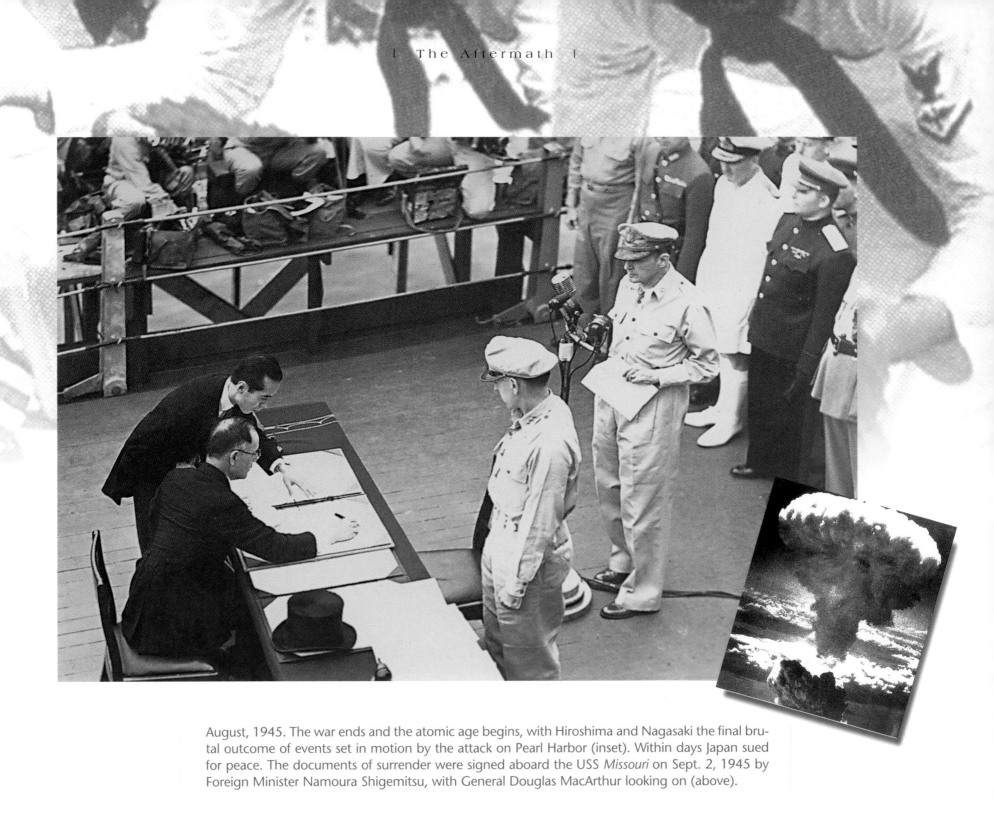

August, 1945. The war ends and the atomic age begins, with Hiroshima and Nagasaki the final brutal outcome of events set in motion by the attack on Pearl Harbor (inset). Within days Japan sued for peace. The documents of surrender were signed aboard the USS *Missouri* on Sept. 2, 1945 by Foreign Minister Namoura Shigemitsu, with General Douglas MacArthur looking on (above).

Despite its disastrous consequences, the attack on Pearl Harbor proved the catalyst that would propel America into war, generating a fervor that played a major role in the restoration and assertion of American power. "Remember Pearl Harbor!" became the rallying cry of government, industry and public opinion during the five years of war that followed the attack on December 7th. This compelling rallying cry committed America to the memory of the 2,341 U.S. servicemen killed on that early Sunday morning.

Japan miscalculated the impact Pearl Harbor would have in focusing the United States energies on all out victory. The production statistics

These Colors WON'T RUN
Remember PEARL HARBOR

"I WANT MY DADDY BACK"

BUY BONDS
"REMEMBER PEARL HARBOR!"

Thanks, Buddy!
NEWSPAPER BOYS HAVE SOLD OVER 1¼ BILLION WAR SAVINGS STAMPS SINCE PEARL HARBOR

THE NAVY NEEDS SHIPS TO
Avenge
PEARL HARBOR
let's go

of the war effort far-out-paced anything over-extended Japan could match. "We are all in it together—all the way," FDR had said to the nation in his weekly fireside chat two days after the attack. "Every single man, woman, and child is a partner in the most tremendous undertaking in our American history."

And so it would be, with big business, big government and big labor all working toward a similar goal. As the "arsenal of democracy" the United States rebuilt its military might to a level that made it pre-eminent in the world, capable of fighting a two front war to victory.

Between Pearl Harbor and Japan's surrender, a timeframe of less than five years, the United States' industry would produce 7,333 ships, 299,000 aircraft, 634,000 jeeps and 88,000 tanks. It was a stupendous outpouring of sustained effort. And behind it all was the phrase "Remember Pearl Harbor," as these wartime posters reveal.

On this anniversary of the attack upon Pearl Harbor let us—

REMEMBER AND HONOR
the men and women who have already given their lives in this struggle.

GIVE THANKS TO GOD
for our survival of the unprovoked attack by ruthless enemies.

TAKE STOCK OF
what we have done in one year of war and what lies ahead to be done in terms of Work-Fight-Sacrifice.

RE-DEDICATE
our strength, time, wealth and our very lives to preserve a concept of living more precious than individual life itself.

For our priceless Bill of Rights and our Constitution of the United States of America we will

WORK! FIGHT! SACRIFICE!

"REMEMBER PEARL HARBOR DAY"
DECEMBER 7, 1942

The Japanese left Hawaiian waters as soon as their planes had landed on the aircraft carriers waiting north of O'ahu. The great Japanese armada was already on its way to its next encounter while a stunned Hawai'i began to deal with the consequences of the attack. With martial law declared, a military layer was added to the role of government in everyday life. Blackout curtains were hung in homes and offices. Gas masks were issued to all civilians. Businesses staggered hours for their workers so as to ease bus transportation problems and accommodate the growing number of war workers. Supplies of consumer goods were often in limited supply since military cargo was given a priority. Soldiers, sailors and pilots were everywhere, a part of the scene from upcountry Wahi'awā to upbeat Waikīkī. In Waikīkī, the navy was a hotelier, having taken over the Royal Hawaiian Hotel as a rest-and-recreation venue

for troops fighting in the Pacific and Asia. As support demands increased, Hawai'i's military population mushroomed to over 135,000—more than double what it had been before the attack. While remaining open to the public, the Moana, Waikīkī's other grand hotel, also hosted military personnel.

Plantation life continued uninterrupted to any large degree by the declaration of war. The Japanese would never seriously challenge American sea lanes, for the war front quickly shifted to the Pacific's scattered islands, coastal Malaya, and the islands of the Dutch East Indies. The flow of supplies between Hawai'i and the Mainland remained open.

The attack on Pearl Harbor was so unexpected and so focused

Within hours of the attack martial law had been declared, making the military a presence in many aspects of daily life (above). Military enlistments were the highest, per capita, in the country. Hawaiian elder Frank Koho, 84, is shown reading instructions for using a gas mask issued by the military to all civilians (right). With the victories that followed Pearl Harbor came the reward of an aloha welcome (below).

on military targets that many were not even aware that an attack had taken place. Even of those who saw the approaching aircraft and heard the explosions that followed were convinced they were no more than realistic battle exercises. But civilians soon learned firsthand that they too might prove to be unanticipated targets, both from enemy fire and from mistimed anti-aircraft weaponry.

After Pearl Harbor, O'ahu was prepared for the possibility of repeat attacks, although reversals for Japan following Pearl Harbor made that less and less likely. Additional gun batteries were positioned near the prow of Diamond Head, and barbed wire was strung along beaches. Large buildings like Aloha Tower and the Dole Cannery were painted in camouflage tones, and gun batteries were covered in camouflage netting. There were restrictions on night lighting, and within weeks of the attack, gas masks

As headquarters for the war in the Pacific, O'ahu was both nerve center and the place to bring war-weary troops for rest and recreation (above). With about 30 percent of the island's population linked to the military, soldiers and sailors were part of the passing parade, particularly in downtown Honolulu and Waikīkī (below).

were issued to all, made mandatory for civilians. The local population willingly cooperated in the effort to protect the Islands from a repeat of the Pearl Harbor disaster. From gasoline rationing to "victory gardens" to voluntary overtime at work, posters in public places emphasized the need to take the war effort personally.

The sayings 'Loose Lips Sink Ships' and 'Rumors Delay Victory' were an indication of the fear that motivated the military to limit civilian access to war-related information after Pearl Harbor.

For Hawai'i's large Japanese-American community the attack was a doubly disturbing event, for it played on underlying fears of the unfamiliar that surface in times of uncertainty and crisis. And while Hawai'i's Japanese were not interned as were Japanese-Americans living along the West Coast, there were attitudes that implied they were under suspicion. No doubt there were those who felt the Japanese Navy could not have launched so secret and successful an attack without some form of complicity by Japanese-Americans, though no such complicity was ever uncovered.

Loyal by cultural tradition and sensitive to the fact that their response would be used to judge whether their loyalty was to the United States, Hawai'i's Japanese joined the military in disproportionate numbers once they were cleared for service in January of 1943. During the war years, Hawai'i boosted the highest enlistment ratt per capita of anyplace in the U.S. The exploits of the all-Japanese-American 442nd Bugade in Europe are legendary.

More than a million Mainlanders would pass through Hawai'i

Hawaiian takes with a military theme. The blend was mostly harmonious. More than one million Mainland GIs would pass through O'ahu during the war years.

comrades-in-arms.

Not all who arrived understood the island lifestyle, and not all local families trusted the unfamiliar outsiders who were now their neighbors. But the nation was not in a divisive mode. Pearl Harbor had identified a common enemy, and war had created a sense of unity focused on victory.

while serving in the military during the war years, almost all of them on O'ahu. Island life adapted to their presence, extending the aloha of

HAWAIIAN LIFE

ON GUARD IN PARADISE
A STORY IN PICTURES

A BRIEF HISTORY OF U.S. DEFENSES IN HAWAII
U.S. NAVY SINCE 1826.   U.S. ARMY SINCE 1898

Searchlights brighten the night sky over Pearl Harbor, circa 1943. By 1943, with Japan on the defensive, fears of a repeat of Pearl Harbor no longer seemed plausible. Like the legendary phoenix, Pearl Harbor would be reborn from the ashes.

CHAPTER EIGHT
·
THE PHOENIX RISES

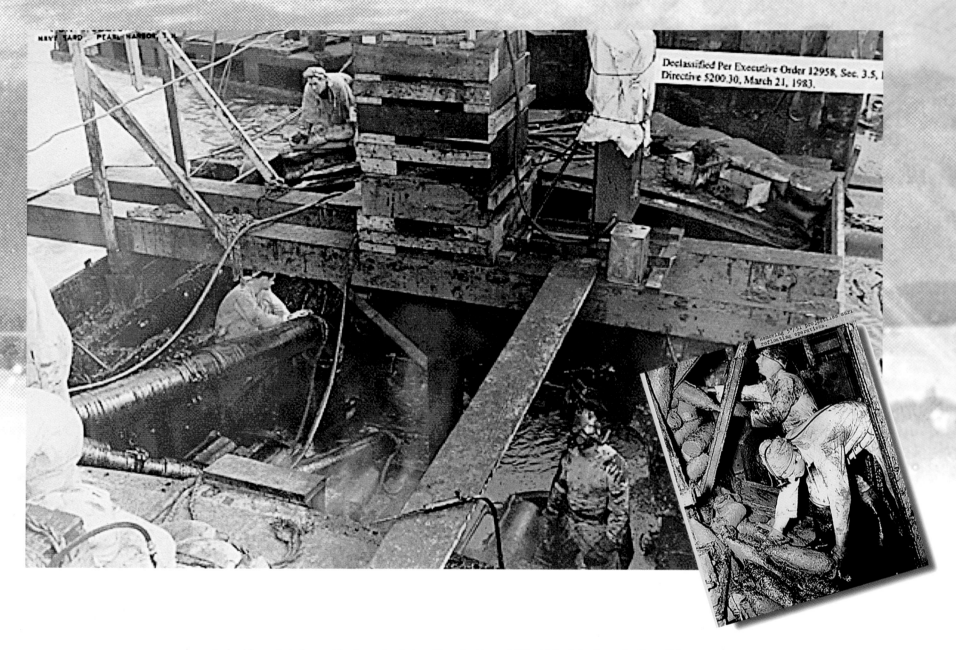

NAVY YARD PEARL HARBOR, T. H.

Declassified Per Executive Order 12958, Sec. 3.5, 1
Directive 5200.30, March 21, 1983.

Removing 3"/51 projection and
reflooting operations.

A dud bomb is found below decks on the shattered *West Virginia* (inset). Conditions during evaluation and salvage were extremely dangerous, with toxic fumes trapped below decks and poisonous chemicals leaking into the harbor (above).

THE PHOENIX RISES

Like the legendary bird rising from the ashes, restored to life in a miracle of rebirth, the U.S. Pacific Fleet and Pearl Harbor's facilities were returned to full strength, with the fleet expanded and defenses upgraded in the process.

A quick appraisal of the damage revealed the losses to be substantial. Eight of the Pacific Fleet's battleships had been hit, some by aerial torpedoes, some by high-altitude bombs, some by a combination of the two. The accuracy of Japanese maps positioning of ships and military installations and the precision with which the pilots hit their targets were impressive accomplishments that made for a successful attack. Both Yamamoto's plan and its execution had been nearly flawless. For the Japanese, the only cause for disappointment and concern was the fact that the American fleet's three aircraft carriers had not been in port. Their survival would give the U.S. response immediate credibility.

Within a few years that bit of good fortune for the Americans proved a disaster for Japan. In battles that would rage at various Pacific locations, the surviving aircraft carriers—the *Saratoga,* the *Lexington,* and the *Enterprise*—would impose impressive defeats on the Japanese fleet. Before the war was through, all the aircraft carriers that had participated in the attack on Pearl Harbor had been destroyed in combat with the Pacific fleet.

The many divers were at high risk, as were the salvage crews probing the fire-scorched, tangled wreckage that had been the Pacific Fleet (below).

But the luck of the carriers had not held for the rest of the U.S. fleet. Three battleships, the *Arizona,* the *Oklahoma,* and the *Utah,* had been sunk. Close to shore, the *Arizona* lay in water to her upper deck. The *Oklahoma* had capsized and lay in the water like a great, beached whale, her rear propeller lamely clear of the water. The *Utah* had sunk in deeper water and was declared a total loss.

The *Nevada* survived the attack and headed toward the harbor entrance. But six direct hits, one torpedo and five bombs, put her at risk. At the command of her captain she was beached well inside the harbor. With subs and midget subs posted outside the harbor entrance, she was saved from likely destruction. Refloated and repaired, the *Nevada* was one the navy's first rebuild success stories.

Heavy losses also applied to the cruisers and destroyers. Four destroyers were hit. The *Cassin,* *Helm* and *Shaw* were ultimately repaired. The *Downes* had to be scrapped, damaged beyond repair. Three light cruisers, one repair ship, one mine-layer, and one seaplane tender also sustained serious damage, although all were eventually returned to service.

Each ship required a careful evaluation as to what might be salvaged and how to restore it to service (above). The destroyer *Downes,* propped up in dry dock, hit by two bombs and further damaged by depth charges and nearby torpedo hits, she was damaged beyond repair. Pearl Harbor Naval Air Station. Not only were planes lost, but all support facilities were badly damaged at Army, Navy, and Marine air installations (inset).

The coordinated effort of military and civilians, men and women, worked to assure Pearl Harbor's security, in this case, stringing barbed wire and working on salvage crews. The salvage effort went on for more than two years.

A portion of the plan to rebuild the *Oklahoma* involved righting her with a long series of electrical winches and steel cables (inset). Work continued, night and day, seven days a week. The *Oklahoma* ultimately proved beyond repair and was decommissioned after salvage efforts were completed in 1945.

Appraising the damage, much of it now below the waterline, meant sending teams of Navy divers into Pearl Harbor's toxic waters. It was a dangerous job, requiring courage, skill, and clear thinking. Each ship was an unknown in terms of the dangers to be encountered. Some were unstable, some burned fuel for days, creating a nightmarish obstacle course of torched interiors.

Pearl's drydock facilities, each with ships under repair, were successfully hit, requiring salvage and rebuilding themselves before the work on the ships could begin. That process of rebuilding took more than a year.

Each ship required a carefully engineered rebuild—custom work of daunting complexity under anything but optimum conditions. Ships had to be moved, some into drydock, dockside, or on-site for repairs that allowed the necessary work to be done.

Some ships had portions cut away in order to reconstruct the ship's framework. Guns and gun turrets had to be removed, interiors cleared, cleaned and rebuilt. Decks needed modifications and rebuilding, guns needed to be reinstalled, ships entirely rewired and replumbed—for the intense heat of the fires that followed the attack melted interiors into fused heaps of melted wreckage. From superstructure to floors, staircases to walls, it was a jigsaw rebuild requiring intelligence and ingenuity.

Damage on the ground was equally dramatic. In total, 164 planes had been destroyed, as well as hangars and maintenance facilities. Six O'ahu bases had been hit, with Wheeler Field's loss of 53 planes the most severe. Twenty-six planes were lost at Ford Island's airstrip.

Repair hardly describes the process of salvage and rebuilding that was required. Pictures report the filthy mix of oil and debris, and that was only the start of the dif-

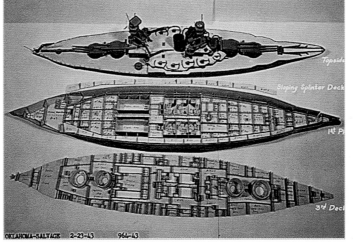

The USS *Cassin* in drydock. It often took years to salvage or repair a damaged ship (inset). A model depiction of the USS *Oklahoma* was used in planning the difficult and damaged salvage of the ship.

ficulties to be faced. There were tangled masses of debris to be navigated and dangerous demolition and clearance tasks to be accomplished by military talent.

With the U.S. now at war, funding Pearl Harbor became a military priority. Fueling a rapid rebuild, government spending and a concerted effort on the part of the Navy and the Army had Pearl up and running at impressive efficiency within a year.

Rebuilding the damaged fleet was a more time-consuming process, however. Parts had to be specially manufactured and delivered, raw materials and equipment shipped in, and crews assembled—including the broad range of specialists required for such a demanding undertaking. By 1943, it was all but a *fait accompli,* with most of the victims of December 7 back in the fleet, ready to even the score. It was an accomplishment made all the more impressive by the parallel challenge facing America in Europe.

America would prove up to the challenge, not just rebuilding the ships that were damaged, but adding dozens of world-class warships and thousands of aircraft to the American arsenal as the war progressed. It was a response that could not be matched by either Germany or Japan, whose explosive successes could not be sustained. ■

The USS *Oklahoma,* hit by more than five torpedoes, lies dead in the water (above). A salvage worker covered in oily grime (inset).

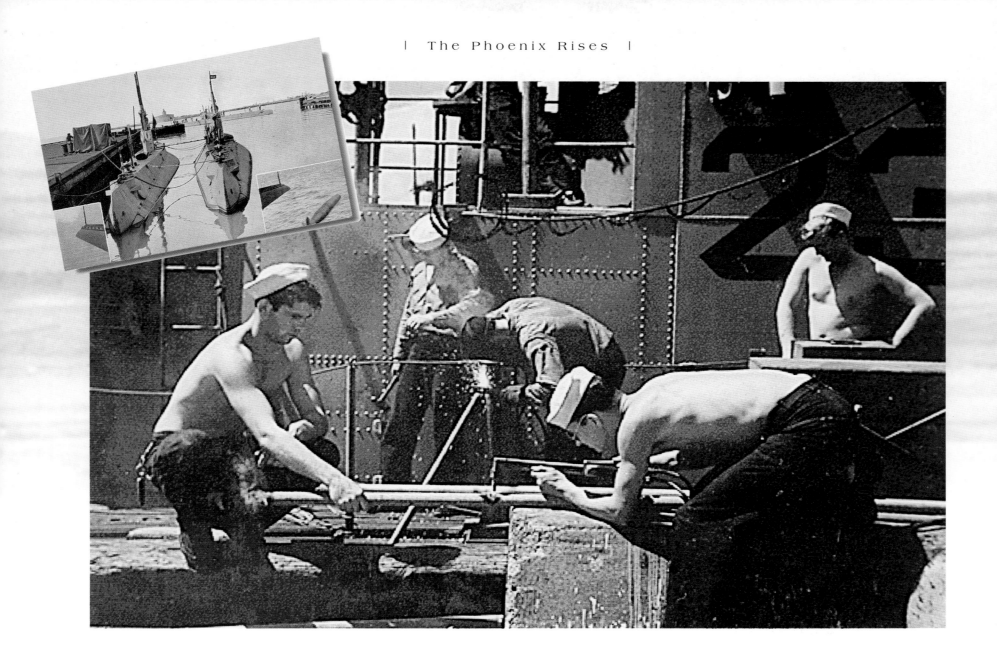

After salvage comes maintenance, a perpetual chore where salt air
and spray are a constant, circa 1944 (above). Submarines at rest at
their Pearl Harbor base, 1943 (inset).

Pearl Harbor, 1943. The Pacific Fleet, rebuilt and expanded, is now fighting a winning war against Japan.

The war ends to fanfare in the streets of downtown Honolulu.

The infamous Japanese attack on Pearl Harbor transforms the romantic island of Hawaii into a living inferno, shatters the lives and loves of three couples, and ends forever America's age of innocence. Starring Angie Dickinson, Dennis Weaver, Robert Wagner and Lesley Ann Warren.

Airing on the ABC Television Network, Thursday, November 16/Friday, November 17/Sunday, November 19, 1978.

As a seminal event in modern American history, and a rallying cry that motivated a generation to exemplary effort, films of the war years often cast a spotlight on Hawai'i and Pearl Harbor. It's a tradition that continues, even as Pearl Harbor drifts further from consciousness and enters the realm of learned history.

The Americans were not alone in making films on the Pearl Harbor theme. For the Japanese it was also a seminal event, a miscalculated effort at righting historic wrongs that made Japan's ultimate victory seem feasible. In fact, the outcome would make curiosities of these cinematic efforts. More propaganda than entertainment, they are also part of the legacy of Pearl Harbor.

Movie posters make epic drama of the Pearl Harbor theme (below). Art for a Japanese-made film on the attack on Pearl Harbor (next page top). A model is prepared for shooting attack scenes.

An aerial view of the East Loch of Pearl Harbor, with the USS *Missouri* and the USS *Arizona* Memorial along the Ford Island shoreline. Oil, still leaking from the tanks of the *Arizona,* rises to the surface in an inky rainbow of color.

CHAPTER NINE
·
PEARL HARBOR TODAY

The silent guns of the USS *Missouri* still impress. The decommissioned battleship has found a final home in Pearl Harbor. It's an appropriate setting, linking the place where the war began with the ship on which it officially drew to a close.

PEARL HARBOR TODAY

Consecrated in violence, Pearl Harbor has become a place of reconciliation and understanding. More than a million people a year pay a visit to the USS *Arizona* Memorial. The National Park Service manages the Visitor Center and Memorial. The U.S. Navy operates the shuttles that take visitors across the waters of Pearl Harbor's East Loch to the *Arizona* Memorial. Now a graceful bridge links Ford Island to the rest of O'ahu. On December 7, all links were by boat.

Before you get to the Memorial, the displays at the Visitor Center's museum provide context for a visit. An inspired 30-minute film follows, providing an objective and riveting account of events, with documentary footage that brings it all to life. When the film ends the theater is silent. Many are damp-eyed; all have been touched. Doors open on a sun-bright world that seems oddly incongruous with the panorama of black clouds and explo-

The USS *Arizona* Memorial Visitor Center, dedicated in 1962, has been operated by the National Park Service since 1980. It lies along Pearl Harbor's eastern shoreline and is part of the Pearl Harbor Naval Station. It offers a not-to-be-missed introduction to the attack on Pearl Harbor.

sive flames that have just raced across the movie screen.

A short narrative accompanies the 15-minute boat trip to the Memorial. There, within a few feet of the Ford Island shoreline, lies the USS *Arizona*, the outline of its upper deck visible through the shallow blue-green of the Pearl Harbor's waters.

The Memorial rises over the *Arizona's* rusting hull. Brilliantly white, it arches toward the heavens, a simple yet exhilarating release from the watery grave it covers. Nearly 1,200 bodies lie below, trapped when the *Arizona* convulsively exploded and sunk. Their names are etched in white marble in a meditation hall at the west end of the rectangular Memorial. Leis and flowers have been left in offering.

Outside, looking down into the water, elements of the upper deck can be seen. Then the silky rainbow of oil on water appears on the surface. The *Arizona* is still releasing oil

The USS *Arizona* Memorial Visitor Center entrance (inset). At the Remembrance Circle, visitors gaze at the tablets that record all of the casualties during the attack on Pearl Harbor (above).

trapped in its hull. The wind makes ripples of the water, and the rainbows fade invisibly into the broad expanse of Pearl Harbor's waters.

Somehow, in the vivid horror of that day comes a deepening of understanding rather than an incitement to hate and anger. It is, after all a humbling experience to realize the extremes that mad is driven. Pearl Harbor has become a place where blame is secondary to understanding.

Still an active military installation and homeport for the Pacific Fleet, Pearl Harbor retains strong links to World War II. There's the USS *Bowfin,* a vintage Second World War submarine that provides an up-close look at what was required to win the war. And there is the impressive scale of the USS *Missouri.* It was aboard the *Missouri* that General Douglas MacArthur officially accepted Japan's surrender, ending the most terrible of all wars. Mighty Mo, as many call her, is an appropriate addition to Pearl Harbor, proclaiming the ultimate victory that would follow what seemed

A casualty list of those lost aboard the *Oklahoma.*

the ultimate disaster. It's a presence that brings closure, affirming that the losses at Pearl Harbor were not without consequences.

Pearl Harbor remains an invaluable asset in America's role as a world power. From Korea through Vietnam, it again served as headquarters of a Pacific Fleet at war.

Could "Pearl Harbor" happen again? Advances in the technology of war have made a naval surprise attack a virtual impossibility. Just as the aircraft carrier supplanted the battleship, so have missiles replaced ships as the method of likely delivery.

It would be a mighty battleship, home to a crew of nearly 1800, that would come to immortalize the events that day and of that time in history. That ship was the USS *Arizona.* Our visit to Pearl Harbor ends here. ■

The vintage World War II submarine, USS *Bowfin,* rests at a dock-side anchorage adjacent to the *Arizona* Memorial Visitor Center.

The explosion-ravaged hull of the USS *Arizona* became a symbol of the trauma inflicted at Pearl Harbor. After it was decided that she was beyond repair, work began removing salvageable parts, including turrets and guns. On December 1, 1942, the *Arizona* was officially removed from the Navy's list of commissioned ships.

Throughout the war and in the immediate post-war years, ships arriving in Pearl Harbor would offer a salute in the *Arizona's* honor. It was not until 1950 that a more formal show of respect was initiated when Admiral Arthur Radford, then Commander of the Pacific Fleet, ordered a flag to be flown from a small platform attached to the *Arizona's* sunken hull.

In 1958, funds were authorized by the U.S. Congress for a more lasting memorial to honor the members of the Armed Forces of the United States who gave their lives to their country during the attack on Pearl Harbor. Additional funds were provided by the State of Hawai'i and several veterans' associations

Work was begun on the project, designed by architect Alfred

Preis, that same year, with the 182-foot memorial dedicated on Memorial Day, 1962. Built entirely above the sunken hull of the *Arizona,* the Memorial rests on concrete pillars sunk into the harbor bottom. There is symbolism in its arching shape, the structure sagging in the center, in defeat, strong and vigorous at the ends, each soaring to ultimate victory.

A Visitor Center, administered by the National Park Service, was completed in 1980. It includes a museum, bookstore and theater, where a 30-minute-long film of gripping intensity is shown. The Navy operates shuttles that take visitors across the East Loch to the site, just off Ford Island.

More than 1.6-million visitors make their way to the USS *Arizona* Memorial each year. It is a shrine with the power to evoke strong emotions, a must-see on just about everyone's itinerary. It is a place to appreciate for its long history and natural beauty as well as for what was suffered here and what was reborn.

The fires extinguished after blazing for two days, the *Arizona* is damaged beyond repair.

The aftermath of attack (above). With guns, turrets and other salvageable parts removed, little of the ship remains above water, although the outline of a portion of the ship and a turret bay are clearly visible (right). The flag flies over the site, part of a small memorial ordered by Admiral Arthur Radford in 1950 (bottom). Work began on a more elaborate memorial in 1958 (left).

An open promenade deck with views of the *Arizona* leads to the memorial chamber where the names of the 1,177 *Arizona* crewmen who perished. Architect Alfred Preis' design arches over the sunken ship, a symbolic reference to the ultimate triumph that followed Pearl Harbor. The *Arizona's* huge anchor stands sentry at the entrance to the visitor center.

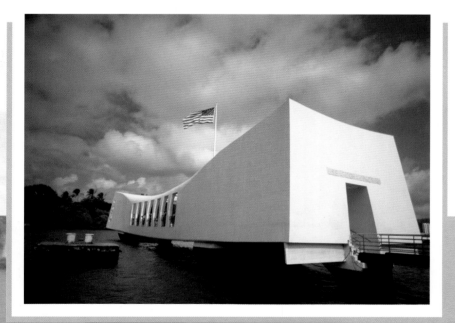

Now in their 70s, these survivors of the attack on Pearl Harbor honor the memory of those lost in the attack by serving as volunteers at the USS *Arizona* Memorial Visitor Center. A word of thanks goes out to Robert Kinzler (above, left) at Schofield Barracks when the planes hit; Everett Hyland (above, middle), aboard the USS *Pennsylvania*, hit in drydock; Albert Alexander (above, right), also at Schofield; Dick Fiske, aboard the *West Virginia* (below, left); and John Haverty, who, at the U.S. Naval Hospital, witnessed a damaged Japanese plane crash into the hospital during the attack (below, right). Volunteers raise and lower flags that are sold to support the USS *Arizona* Memorial Museum Association.

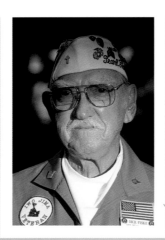 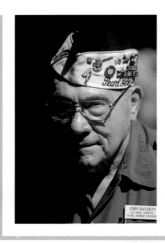 

A Navy launch approaches the USS *Arizona* Memorial, a place of remembrance and reflection. Those honored here, most lost to a watery grave, have their memory preserved, a symbol of the brutal reality of war.

BIBLIOGRAPHY

Albright, Harry. *Pearl Harbor—Japan's Fatal Blunder,* New York: Hippocrene Books, 1988.

Arakakai, Leatrice, John R. Kuborn. *7 December 1941: The Air Force Story,* Hickam Air Base, Hawai'i: Pacific Air Force Office of History, 1991.

Delgado, James P. *Pearl Harbor Recalled,* Annapolis, Maryland: Naval Institute Press, 1991.

Goldstein, Donald M., Katherine Dillon, and J. Michael Wenger. *Pearl Harbor,* Washington: Brassey's, 1995.

Hudson, Robert Stephen. *Sunrise, Sunset: December 7, 1941,* Honolulu: R.S. Hudson, 1986.

Kamakau, Samuel. *The Works of the People of Old,* Honolulu: Bishop Museum Press, 1976.

Kimmett, Larry, and Margaret Regis. *The Attack on Pearl Harbor,* Seattle: Navigator Publishing, 1999.

Kuykendall, R.S. *The Hawaiian Kingdom,* Vol. 2, 3, Honolulu: University of Hawai'i Press, 1953.

Smith, Carl. *Pearl Harbor,* Oxford, England: Osprey History, 1999.

Summers, T. *Hawaiian Fishponds,* Honolulu: P.B. Bishop Museum Special Publication #52, 1976

Taylor, Theodore. *Air Raid—Pearl Harbor!,* New York: Thomas Y. Crowell, 1971.

Toland, John. *Infamy: Pearl Harbor and its Aftermath,* New York: Doubleday, Garden City, 1982

Travers, Paul Joseph. *Eyewitness to Infamy, An Oral History of Pearl Harbor,* New York: Madison Books, 1991.

Trefousse, Hans L. *Pearl Harbor: The Continuing Controversy,* Malabar Florida: Rob't. Krieger Pub. Co., 1982.

Winiewski, Richard A. *Pearl Harbor and the USS Arizona Memorial:* A Pictorial History, Honolulu: Pacific Basin Enterprises, 1977

Wohlstetter, Roberta. *Pearl Harbor Warning and Decision,* Stanford, California: Stanford University Press, 1962.

PHOTO CREDITS

The pictures used in this book have been carefully selected from the following archival sources:

Hawaiian Legacy Archive
P.2, p.3 all; p. 5 all; p. 6-7; p. 9 top; p. 10 all; p. 11 all; p.12 all; p.13 all; p. 14; p.19 top; p. 20 center, left; p. 21 right; p.22 left; p. 23 bottom; p.29; p. 31 all; p.32 left; p.35 all; 49 bottom; p. 51 bottom; p. 52 top; p. 53 bottom; p. 55 left, right; p.56 all; p. 57 all; p. 82 all; p. 83 all; p. 84 all; p. 85 right. top; p. 86 all p. 87 all; p. 88-89; p. 100 (collection Daniel Martinez); p. 102 Desoto Brown Collection; p. 103 bottom left; p. 117 background.

Allan Seiden
p. 104-105 all; p. 106; p. 107 all; p. 108 all; p. 109 all; p.110-111; 110 all; p. 114 all; p. 115 all; p. 116; p. 112-113.

USS _Arizona_ Memorial/NPS, Photo Collection
Works by Tom Freeman: p. 14, background; p. 24-25; p. 27 top; p. 34-35 background; 38-39; p.41 top; p. 44 all; p. 48 center; p. 52 inset; right; p. 54 inset; p. 58 inset above; p. 58-59 background. Archival: p. 1 top; p. 22; p. 34 bottom; p. 36 bottom; p. 37 top right; p. 40 inset; p. 43 all; p. 45 right; p. 54; p. 59 bottom; p. 60-61 all; p. 63 bottom; p.64 center; p. 65; p. 69 inset; p. 79 inset; p. 92 center; p. 95 bottom right; p. 103 bottom right; p. 112; p. 113 bottom, left.

The National Archive
p. 20 top; p.22 center; p. 26 inset; p. 28; p. 30; p.31; p. 33 center; p. 34 top; p. 35 top, bottom ; p.36 top; p. 37 left top, bottom; p.40 all; p. 42 center; p. 45 center; p. 46 inset; p. 49 inset; p. 51 center, inset; p.52; p. 59 top, both; p. 62; p. 63 top; p. 64 inset; p. 66 all; p. 67all; p. 73; p. 74; p. 76 top, bottom; p. 77 all; p. 78 all; p. 80 all; p. 81 all; p. 90 all; ; p. 91 all; p. 92 top; p. 94 all; p 95 center; p. 96 center; p. 97 all; p. 102-103 background; p. 103 bottom right; p. 112 bottom; p. 113 top; p. 119 all; p. 117 bottom.

US Navy
p. 50 center; p. 55 center; p. 58 bottom; p.72.

The Bishop Museum
p. X-1; p. 4; p. 16-17; p. 23 center

Hawai'i State Archives
p. 8, Hawai'i State Archives, Fuhrman Collection; p. 12-13 background; p. 15; p. 18; p. 19 bottom; p. 21center; p.23 top; p. 37 right bottom; p. 42 top; p. 46; p. 48 inset; p. 49 center; p. 50 inset; p. 53; p. 68 all; p. 69 Fuhrman Collection; p. 70-71; p. 75; p. 76 center; p. 79 center; p. 85 bottom; p. 93 top; p. 96 inset; p. 98; p. 113 right.

University of Hawai'i
p. 51 inset; p. 53 top; p. 99;

DeSoto Brown Collection
p. 102, two center; p. 103 top.

Herb Kāne
p. 9 bottom.

United States Army Museum Hawai'i
p. 26; p. 27; p. 30 inset; p. 33 right; p. 41 bottom; p. 42 bottom right; p. 93 center.